Welsh History

Strange but True

*This book is dedicated to all the people of Wales.
Without their unwavering commitment
to oddness and peculiarity,
this book would never have been written.*

Welsh history

Strange but True

Geoff Brookes

About the Author

GEOFF BROOKES is a writer with a long-standing interest in Welsh history. His previous books include *Bloody Welsh History: Swansea*, *Swansea Then & Now* and *Swansea Murders*. He has appeared in *The Times Education Supplement* and *Welsh Country Magazine*, as well as in a range of other publications, such as the *Independent*. He lives in Swansea.

First published 2014, this edition 2017

The History Press
The Mill, Brimscombe Port
Stroud, Gloucestershire, GL5 2QG
www.thehistorypress.co.uk

British Library Cataloguing in Publication Data.
A catalogue record for this book is available from the British Library.

ISBN 978 0 7509 8342 6

Typesetting and origination by The History Press

Contents

Preface

There is a story which may not be true. It might only be an urban myth, which would be a great shame because it deserves to be a true slice of life. It tells of a man – in some versions it is the actor Anthony Hopkins – who takes a cab in New York.

'Where are you from?' asks the driver.

'Wales.'

'And Wales is what exactly? A big fish, Diana's husband or them singing bastards?'

A tough choice, I think. But what this book intends to show is that the Welsh are not all singing bastards.

Some are a whole lot worse.

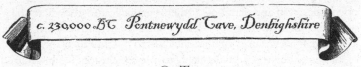
On Tour

Neanderthal remains have been found in Pontnewydd Cave in Denbighshire, near St Asaph. They were dated in 1981 and were confirmed as being about 230,000 years old – the oldest remains ever uncovered in Wales. A total of nineteen teeth were found, coming from five different individuals, both children and adults. One piece of jawbone holding a milk tooth and a permanent molar are believed to have come from an 11-year-old boy. There were also some stone tools and animal bones in the cave.

The teeth could, of course, be all that is left of an ancient burial site, scoured in the intervening millennia by retreating ice sheets. They had been there an awfully long time. Alternatively, it was the site of an early dental clinic.

Neanderthals are a particular branch of the evolutionary tree – and one of nature's less attractive experiments. We shared a common ancestor with them but did not evolve from them. They had sloping foreheads, large brow ridges, big square jaws, short limbs, and they were pug-ugly. They were hunters who needed to get close to their prey in order to catch them, since they do not appear to have developed the use of weapons. They must have attacked in packs, showing a level

+ A stone hand axe found in Rhosili was made by a Neanderthal craftsman about 100,000 years ago.

+ The earliest inhabitants of Cardiff left behind the Pen-y-Lan hand axe, dating from 75,000 BC.

+ The hardest and most time-consuming part of making an axe head was boring a hole all the way through the stone or flint for a handle, using only wood, stone and sand.

+ In 2006 a professor from Oxford University suggested that bachelor twins from Strata Florida were the last carriers of the Neanderthal bloodline. Every year children from Tregaron School were taken up to meet them as part of their study of evolution. Sadly the twins left no photographs.

of co-operation and planning. Other remains found elsewhere show signs that their hunting style left some of them with broken limbs. They did, however, use simple stone tools to butcher their meat.

All this evidence points inevitably to one conclusion. Teeth scattered everywhere? Broken limbs? Close-proximity fighting? A distinctive evolutionary branch? The Neanderthal party that left their teeth in Pontnewydd were nothing more complicated than a rugby team on tour who were looking for the local sport injuries clinic.

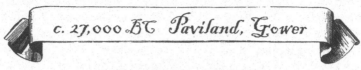

c. 27,000 BC Paviland, Gower

The Red Lady of Paviland

Let's get one thing straight before we start. The Red Lady of Paviland was no lady. She was a man.

Bones, believed to be those of elephants, had been found in December 1822. The discovery brought William Buckland, Professor of Geology at Oxford University, to the site in Goat's Hole in January 1823 and he unearthed the remains of an incomplete skeleton, stained red. The bones were from the right side of the body.

The other bones that must have been there were probably disturbed by the action of the sea over the centuries. The area around the body, along with the bones themselves, was stained red. So were the items buried with the body – mammoth ivory bracelet fragments and perforated periwinkle shells. There were also small limestone blocks that may have been placed at the head and feet. Perhaps the skull of a mammoth found nearby may have also been part of the burial ritual. Sadly the skull has since been lost.

When Buckland published his findings later in the year he had decided that the ochre-stained skeleton was a 'painted lady' who entertained the Roman soldiers garrisoned in the camp on the hill above the cave. Alternatively, she could have been a witch.

The problem was Buckland was entirely wrong: the burial was male, and the mammoth products were original and Palaeolithic and not manufactured in some way at a later date as decorations. The camp was Iron Age, not Roman.

We now believe that the Red Lady was a ceremonial Palaeolithic burial dating from about 27,000 BC. The Red Lady was a healthy young adult male, aged between 25 and 30, about 5ft 6in tall and weighing about 11 stones. The head of the Red Lady has never been found, though it may have been removed as part of a burial ritual. There are other examples of this in similar graves from the period.

The find, though, was enormously significant. The Red Lady was the first human fossil found anywhere in the world – and is still the oldest ceremonial burial uncovered in Western Europe.

✦ William Buckland found it very hard to date his prehistoric find in Paviland with any accuracy. He refused to believe that anything could pre-date the notional date of Noah and the Great Flood.

---

c. 12,000 BC Llandudno

Mr Kendrick's Mandible

Thomas Kendrick had been employed in the local copper mines in Llandudno as a stonemason, but by 1880 he had retired and was working as a lapidary, making cheap jewellery from seaside pebbles. Even in the nineteenth century the idea of taking home meaningless souvenirs from the seaside was well established, and Mr Kendrick was eager to do whatever he could to relieve tourists of their unwanted cash.

He was working in his garden at his house Ardwy Orme on the Great Orme, clearing a small natural cave in order to extend his workshop. The cave was about 50ft deep and 16ft wide. Whilst the view from his garden of the promenade below him was impressive, it would soon pale into insignificance in comparison with what he discovered in the cave. Because he uncovered a significant treasure of prehistoric art, including a decorated horse jaw with three remaining incisor teeth, the oldest piece of portable art from Wales ever discovered.

The cave was probably a burial site. There were flint artefacts, animal teeth which had been pierced to use as jewellery, eight types of mollusc and human bones from three adults and a teenager. They had been nomadic hunters, probably from mainland Europe. The objects buried with them appear to have been coloured with ochre, just like those from Paviland. The find dated from about 12,000 BC. The jaw was decorated with zigzag lines and disappeared for a long time, until it was delivered to the British Museum in 1959.

Further discoveries were made in the twentieth century when the cave was excavated again, but the fear has always been that other objects were lost in earlier times. In this way the contents of the cave always give a tantalising – and frustrating – hint of the treasures that once might have been there.

+ The outline of a reindeer carved into the wall of Cathole Cave in Gower is the oldest piece of rock art found so far in Britain, possibly in North Western Europe at 14,000 years old. It was etched with a flint by an artist using their right hand.

+ Bacon Cave in Gower was named because of the ten red-coloured bands that initially were identified as examples of Palaeolithic art. It was not, however, the artist's homage to a packet of streaky. It was merely red oxide mineral seeping through the rock.

+ At Penywyrlod near Talgarth in Powys the perforated leg bone of a sheep was found, dating from about 3650 BC. Holes appear to have been deliberately cut to make a whistle. Of course, the holes could have been made by gnawing animals, but it is nice to think that Welsh musical heritage has such a long history.

+ A woman's body was excavated at Llandegai in Anglesey dating from before 2000 BC which had been buried in a bag of animal skin.

+ In 1833, workmen dug a hole beside the Chester to Mold Road (nowadays known as the A541). They found part of a skeleton and the largest single gold item ever found in Britain – the Mold Cape, dating from about 1900 BC. It was a single sheet of beaten gold, decorated with amber beads and made to cover the shoulders and upper body.

+ The Presaddfed Burial Chamber at Bodedern in Anglesey is said to have been used as a home by a family in the eighteenth century.

+ At Brenig in Denbighshire, a Bronze Age child aged around 6 months was found cremated and buried in an urn.

+ One single charred pea, found in excavations in Church Street, Carmarthen, is the only evidence of a legume anywhere in South West Wales.

+ A mattock made from an antler from a red deer was found in 1992, lying on the clay in front of the Uskmouth power station. It had been used for digging, possibly in the search for cockles. It was found close to human footprints, preserved in the silt which is exposed at low tide. Three trails of prints dating from 4000 BC were recorded. Two were those of adult males, shoe sizes 8 and 9. The third trail belonged to a child. Footprints have also been found at Magor Pill and Goldcliff.

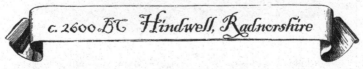

c. 2600 BC **Hindwell, Radnorshire**

Wood You Believe It?

There is a faint but remarkable outline on the land in Radnorshire. At Hindwell there is the shadow of an enormous wooden enclosure, built between 2700 and 2500 BC. It is so old that not even the Romans would have known it was ever there. It had long gone by the time they arrived. Only modern aerial photography revealed its presence in 1992. And yet no one really knows what it was for.

The enclosure was oval shaped and formed by timber posts to create some kind of enormous stockade. The scale is staggering. There were 1,400 posts, each nearly 2ft in diameter and probably 20ft tall. The circumference is just about 2.5km and it enclosed a space of 34 hectares, the area of 55 football pitches, apparently. If the gaps between the carefully spaced posts had been filled with timber, as they probably were, then they would have used an additional 12,000 tons of wood.

+ Whatever Stonehenge might be – a burial site, a temple for sun worship, a healing centre, a huge calendar – the bluestones towards the centre of the monument appear to have come from the Presceli Hills in Pembrokeshire. How and why they were transported to Wiltshire remains unclear. There is evidence of cattle being driven from Wales to Wiltshire. Perhaps cattle were used to haul the bluestones for Stonehenge from Presceli.

+ Rhondda has its own 'Stonehenge' – Mynydd y Gelli, an arrangement of scattered stones in a rough circle. It is next to a landfill site.

It would have taken a long time to build and used up a vast amount of the local resources. Estimates suggest that 23 hectares of woodland would have had to be felled. The easiest way would have been to build a fire around the base of the trees and burn them through. But they would still have had to remove side branches and trim them, all with stone axes. The Hindwell enclosure would have taken over three years to build. There were pits to dig for the posts, which would have to be dragged into position (perhaps by cattle) and then carefully planted. It would have taken huge dedication to construct something on this scale, which would dwarf anything any of the people would ever have seen before. It had a narrow entrance 2m wide, which might suggest that it was built to facilitate entry in ceremonial procession. But its purpose remains a mystery.

The whole area is crawling with prehistoric remains. It always had a strategic importance, lying between the hills of Central Wales and the English Midlands, something which the Romans acknowledged by building a fortress there themselves. But they would not have seen Hindwell. Even if it survived intact for 200 years – which is unlikely – it had disappeared over 2,000 years before they turned up.

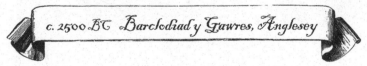

c. 2500 BC *Barclodiad y Gawres, Anglesey*

'Fire Burn and Cauldron Bubble'

There is a Neolithic burial chamber on the southern coast of Anglesey, in a beautiful setting on Mynydd Cnwc, overlooking Porth Trecastell. Called Barclodiad y Gawres, it is an example of a cruciform passage grave and is noted for its decorated stones. It is very similar to graves across the sea in Ireland and the decorative patterns are like those found in Llandudno.

The site was built at about the same time as the Pyramids, though to a more modest design. It was excavated in 1952 and rebuilt to resemble its original layout, protected now by a large concrete dome. The excavations revealed two cremated young males in one of the side rooms. In the central part of the tomb there were the remains of a fire, on to which had been poured a stew as some kind of offering or magical potion. The recipe appears to have come straight from the

witches' cookbook as used in *Macbeth*. The ingredients? Wrasse, eel, frog, toad, grass snake, mouse, shrew and hare. It was then covered with limpet shells and pebbles. If it wasn't an offering, then perhaps it was a warming winter casserole that went horribly wrong. Perhaps it needed a touch more garlic.

The more prosaic explanation is that this infernal stew is in fact the remains of an otter's toilet – he'd moved in for a while – but let's not let historical accuracy snatch away all our dreams.

The name of the burial chamber translates as 'Apronful of the Giantess' and to be honest, whatever this pile of inedible refuse might once have been, you certainly wouldn't want it in your apron.

- The first pieces of jewellery found in Wales were perforated sea shells and strings of stone beads.

- Possessions were few, and valuable. Perhaps this is why the Welsh didn't often bury their dead with objects from everyday life.

- In 2012, remains of a wooden structure were found outside Monmouth, which may have been a Neolithic longhouse or hall.

1700 BC Llandudno

Earth, Water, Fire and Air

Mining in Wales is not a modern phenomenon at all. It has a very long history. In the nineteenth century, when Welsh copper strengthened the hulls of British warships and produced the currency that lubricated the slave trade, miners discovered that they were not the first men beneath the ground. Miners on the Great Orme frequently uncovered old tunnels containing bone tools. Some of the tunnels they found were so small that they could only have been worked by children – minors as miners. Their tools came from cattle. Ribs and legs provided picks and shoulder blades were used as shovels. In fact at least 33,000 digging bones have been found there.

Modern scientific techniques have shown that the mines had been worked for thousands of years. By about 1700 BC the copper ore mines on the Great Orme on the North Wales coast together formed the largest mine in Europe. It began as an open-cast operation which removed about 28,000 tons of rock in pursuit of the copper ore. Soon they followed the seams underground, digging tunnels with bone tools. Fires would be burnt against the rock surface to weaken it and in doing so created horrible working conditions.

The ore had to be separated from the rock. Much was sorted by hand and then washed to remove limestone. The temperatures required to

smelt the recovered copper ore were achieved by using hand bellows and charcoal which put great strain on local woodland resources. It was a sophisticated operation which required judgement and skill. They used tin sourced from Cornwall to make bronze, further proof that these were not insular communities; trade was a vital part of life at this time.

Mining had also been going on in Mynydd Parys on Anglesey for some time. Research suggests that miners reached a depth of 30m by 1900 BC. There were other sites too, across Wales.

It is strange but true that DNA testing of some current residents in Abergele suggests strong links with the early inhabitants of Spain, where mining was already well established by 1900 BC. Perhaps the miners who settled at the foot of the Great Orme in prehistoric times had relocated from Spain as immigrant workers.

+ Communities at this time were not completely isolated. There was extensive trading. Stone axes made in Wales have been found in Dorset and the Isle of Man. Items made from Cornish rocks have been found in Wales.

+ At Porth Neigwl on the Llyn Peninsula there was fertile land that extended into the Irish Sea – though it was subsequently lost to the tides.

+ The remains of the many different kinds of animal have been discovered in Wales. They include bears, reindeer, elk, ibexes, bison, mammoth, hyenas and lynx.

+ A mace head carefully carved from flint and intricately decorated was found at Maesnor in Denbighshire. It is thought that it was used for ceremonial purposes.

Gold was less important to the Welsh than copper. It is a soft metal and in a practical subsistence society, that limits the uses to which it can be put. So while the rest of Europe was getting excited about gold jewellery, in Wales they were still more concerned with chopping and shaping.

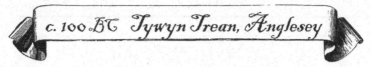

c. 100 BC   Tywyn Trean, Anglesey

The Llyn Cerrig Bach Hoard

Of course, they are much more sophisticated in the north than those of us in the south. Just look at what they threw into their peaty water – swords, bracelets … all we can ever manage to throw into our rivers are supermarket trolleys.

It has become known as the Llyn Cerrig Bach Hoard and was made up of 181 bronze and iron objects. It is one of the greatest treasures from the Iron Age and was found by accident in 1942, during the construction of RAF Valley airfield.

The soil was sandy and the American Flying Fortress bombers to be stationed there were heavy, so they extracted peat from the bogs to stabilise the sand. As the peat was removed, metal objects and bones emerged. A 3m-long chain was uncovered early on and it was used for a time to drag out lorries that were stuck in the mud. In fact it wasn't an old farm chain, as the contractors first believed. It was an ancient gang chain over 2,000 years old, intended to link together a group of slaves with neck collars. There were chariot fittings, swords, cauldrons, tools and bracelets. They were probably offerings to the water gods, a practice that the Celts were very keen on.

The discovery was, of course, bad timing. Wartime priorities were far more important than archaeological precision. It is believed that some items were never identified and still lie beneath the tarmac of the runway.

There was a small cliff from which the offerings were thrown into the lake for the gods. It was known as Craig y Carnnau (the Rock of the Hooves). Now it is known less romantically as TACAN Hill (Tactical Air Navigation) and is now inaccessible.

Scoff as we might about the strange disposal of treasures, people today can't resist hurling small change into fountains and wells. We are no different in our deep-seated need to propitiate the water spirits than our Celtic ancestors.

> ✦ A piece of a lead anchor found off the Llyn Peninsula has been
> identified as coming from a second century sea-going vessel
> from the Mediterranean. Even before the first official contact,
> Roman traders and merchants had been visiting Britain,
> searching for opportunities ...

AD 1 Wales

The Lost Secrets of Atlantis?

The traditional image of the Druids – long flowing hair, white robes, serious wisdom, a sense of mania – is all part of a nineteenth-century invention. The reality is a lot less clear. Certainly the Druids were seen as a significant threat by the Romans, not perhaps for what they were but rather for what they represented. Essentially they were the priestly brotherhood of the Celts.

The Druids didn't have any formal family of gods whom they worshipped. They seemed to have offered their devotion to natural things, like oak trees and mistletoe. Their sacred places were usually in woods or groves. In Celtic society, they were the only ones allowed to carry out rituals and ceremonies. They had been chosen for this role at birth and had been initiated into its mysteries. These stories and beliefs were the things that brought the disparate tribes of Wales together; they may have inhibited the Welsh from fighting each other, but certainly gave them the inclination to confront the Romans. Druidism has been described as the earliest native spirituality of Britain, though no one can be quite sure what it was, except that the Romans didn't like it. The Druids were responsible for preserving the tribal myths, for they could never be written down in a culture which possessed no writing. It was the Druids and the Bards who passed on traditions to the next generation.

However, there are no archaeological finds anywhere that could be described as Druidic. It has been an entirely oral tradition which has been passed down and as a result has seeped into the national consciousness and brought myths to itself like a magnet for weird things. You can, if you wish, persuade yourself that the Druids are the inheritors of the spiritual beliefs of Atlantis. And they might

well be – it is just that no one can be sure what those spiritual beliefs were.

Druidism has absorbed lots of strange and disparate beliefs though the centuries but, when they are squeezed out, no one can be at all sure what has been left behind.

 AD 40 Wales

At Home in the Iron Age

Julius Caesar described Britain as a land of small farms, and Wales in the Iron Age was no different. Subsistence farming had been fairly successful for thousands of years, allowing for a gradual increase in the population. It was a period of enormous change. People started to live in larger communities and showed more interest in their appearance and personal adornment. Strangely, it was the need to pay Roman taxes that changed a way of life forever. They had to be more productive as a matter of urgency so that they could pay their taxes, either in kind or in cash. A simple and balanced way of life was lost forever.

Mixed agriculture was practised, mainly cereal production and the keeping of livestock. Most people had pigs and sheep and goats, but cattle were by far the most important. They provided heavy farm labour as well as manure, hide, milk and food. Chickens were introduced shortly before the Romans arrived. People grew wheat, especially spelt. Barley was grown everywhere. Grain was stored in granaries which were raised above ground or in pits underground.

> ✦ None of the tribes that inhabited Wales in the Iron Age produced their own coins. The ones that have been found came from other parts of Britain and Europe.
>
> ✦ What is possibly the oldest human portrait from Wales can be seen on a fragment from a brass shield (dated *c.* 50 BC) found on the slopes of Cader Idris, overlooking Tal-y-llyn lake in 1963.

Iron Age people made bread and porridge from the cereals and beer from the barley. They would remove the surface foam (or yeast) from the fermenting beer and add it to their bread mix. Limited evidence has been found of oats and rye or of vegetables. They seem to have supplemented their diet with nuts and berries, honey, leaves, flowers and roots. They ate wild animals that they hunted with dogs, fish and birds.

Families lived in conical huts, which provided excellent warmth and shelter. The smoke from the central open fire found its way through the thatch. It provided light and was maintained twenty-four hours a day. In the roof space they hung meat and fish to smoke, their only means of food preservation. In West Wales they also hung up their coracles so that the smoke and tar deposits from the fire would help to waterproof them. Beds were raised above the ground and covered with animal skins.

The Roman invasion had a significant impact upon this uncomplicated way of life. There was an army of occupation to support, after all.

 AD 43 Kent

Here Come the Romans

The Romans landed in Kent in AD 43 and fought their way to the River Severn in AD 48. To the north, campaigns a year earlier led by Ostorius Scapula defeated the Cornovii, who lived in Cheshire and Shropshire. As the Romans moved deeper into Wales, the greatest resistance came from the Silures in the south, which is why the largest number of forts was built there.

Slowly the Welsh tribes became integrated into the Roman way of life – or at least as much as they needed to, here at the edge of the Empire. But the advantages were there for all to see: prosperity, order and progress.

THP

But it wasn't all plain sailing. The Ordovices rebelled against Roman occupation between AD 70 and AD 80, foolishly destroying a cavalry squadron of about 120 mounted troops. In response the governor, Agricola, went up into the hills to get them. He is said to have exterminated the tribe – a threat levelled against the Silures but never carried out. If he succeeded isn't clear – and of course, parts of central Wales are a little inaccessible – but certainly the Ordovices never appear again in the written record after AD 78. A lost tribe perhaps.

The Silures didn't go quietly either. They conducted a resistance based upon guerrilla war tactics, picking off small parties of

Romans whenever they could. They took Roman soldiers as hostages and distributed them amongst the other tribes to increase resistance. In fact it is believed that they destroyed an entire legion in AD 52. Scapula himself said that they were such a danger that they should be either entirely destroyed or relocated. He had already squashed the Deceangli and was ready to have a go at Anglesey, but was called away to deal with the Brigantes in the north, who were causing trouble. The Silures were eventually subdued by Sextus Julius Frontinus in AD 78. No one knows how. The historian Tacitus described them as influenced neither by cruelty nor by clemency – perhaps they reached an agreement, or perhaps they were defeated.

+ Verica, the chieftain of the Atrebatic tribe, asked for assistance from the Romans in confronting the Catuvellauni. This was the excuse the Romans used to invade Britain in AD 43.

+ There were six significant tribes in Wales at the beginning of the Roman invasion – the Silures who lived in the south, the Demetae in the south-west, the Cornovii and the Dobunni in the east, the Ordovices in central Wales and the Deceangli in the north.

+ The Romans regarded Wales with a mixture of fascination and indifference. It was distant enough (at the edge of civilization) to be exotic, but few individuals ever made any impact on the history of the Empire.

+ The Silure tribe are described as having a dark complexion and curly hair. The Romans believed that they were immigrants from Spain.

+ The name Cornovii may mean that the tribe worshipped a horned god. At Abbots Bromley, a village in Staffordshire which is in the Cornovii territory, there is an annual horn dance which is a pagan ritual.

+ The Romans were quick to exploit the mineral wealth of Wales, which was one of their reasons for invasion. They were soon mining Welsh lead and silver to such an extent that Spanish producers complained that they were being undercut and priced out of the market.

Roaming

Caratacus or Caractacus, known to the Welsh as Caradog, was the son of Cunobelinus, a chieftain of the Catuvellauni tribe in south-east Britain (a rather difficult bunch, it has to be said). They certainly didn't take too kindly to the appearance of the Roman army.

After their defeat at the Battle of the Medway when his brother Togodumnus was killed, Caratacus and his tribe fled to South Wales, where he became a rallying point for resistance against the Roman occupation. As such, he was someone the Romans were anxious to destroy and a reason why they decided to invade Wales.

He went first to the Silures and later retreated into mid-Wales, where the Catuvellauni fought alongside the Ordovices. They were defeated, however, in AD 51 at the Battle of Caer Caradog by the 14th and 20th Legions. Caratacus fled to the north of Britain.

He tried to take refuge amongst the Brigantes, who didn't really need to be part of his feud. Their queen, Cartimandua, betrayed him to the Romans. He had evaded capture for over seven years.

He was taken to Rome for ritual and triumphant execution in the same way as the great Gaulish leader Vercingetorix, who was garrotted.

Caratacus was paraded through Rome with his family, and his notoriety brought out crowds to see him. The historian Tacitus described him as the man 'who for so many years had spurned our power' (Tacitus, *The Annals*). He even dared to address Emperor Claudius as an equal, though to be frank by now he had little to lose. He suggested that in other circumstances he could have come to Rome as an ally and cleverly argued that to spare him would bring Claudius credit and renown. If he were to be executed the emperor would quickly be forgotten, a lost footnote in history.

Claudius was so impressed by his bravery and oratory that he granted him his life and the promise that he could live in respected and honoured retirement – but in Rome, not in Wales. Subduing the Welsh tribes was a significant drain on resources and Caratacus would not have been an asset.

AD 53 Caerwent

Haec Est Nostra Mundi

The Romans did not rule through the military. The army was naturally responsible for the initial conquest and the suppression of the natives, but Roman rule was sustained by an efficient administration. Power was delegated through the government of the province to regional capitals. These capitals brought Roman rule across the surrounding area and took responsibility for the roads, which were of huge importance.

The roads created a network of trade routes. Towns grew up where the roads met or where bridges crossed a river. It was trade that in reality defined the Empire, and the Roman roads that held it all together.

The towns that they built must have been such a shock to the people of Wales. When the Romans conquered the rest of the world they took control of existing towns – but not in Wales. They took over tribal areas. As a result the towns in Wales, however small they were, had a huge symbolic impact in a country where nothing like this had ever existed before. The towns provided a social focus – for gathering together, for social events, rituals, a sense of community. The Welsh saw other things too. Roman soldiers could retire after twenty-five years' service in the army. They were given land and a

+ The important settlement of Caerwent was known as *Venta Silurium*. The modern translation of *Venta* is 'market'.

+ There was an inn at Caerwent that provided baths, food, a bed and probably fresh horses for messengers on official business.

+ Caerwent has the best-preserved urban defences of any Roman town in Britain.

+ One of the most important instruments used by Roman town planners was the 'groma' – a simple theodolite.

+ The foundations of a first-century fort were found in Cardiff beneath the castle in the city centre. The Normans used materials from the Roman castle to build their own.

+ Neath Abbey was built in the twelfth century using stone from the ruined Roman fortress.

+ A regiment of 500 Spanish cavalrymen was based at Cicutium (Y Gaer, near Brecon). Roman stones from Y Gaer were used by the Normans in 1090 to build Brecon Castle.

+ All Roman forts were built to an identical pattern so that troops, even if new arrivals, would know what to do in the event of an attack.

+ The Mediterranean style of house – four wings around a small internal courtyard with gulleys to collect the rainwater – never caught on in Roman Wales. Too much rain swamped the drains.

+ *Aedile* was the name given to the Roman official who dealt with public services, such as water supply.

+ Bathing was regarded as an essential activity by Roman settlers. It was a new concept entirely to Welsh tribes.

+ There were four separate sections to a Roman bathhouse – the *frigidarium* (cold bath), *tepidarium* (warm bath) *caldarium* (hot bath) and the *paleastra* (exercise hall).

+ Seneca, the Roman dramatist, lived above some public baths in Rome and often raged about the shouting of customers who were having their nasal hairs plucked.

+ Romans were always complaining about the standard of home repairs, because they felt they were in danger from falling tiles and masonry.

house for their families. This promoted the growth of towns and also provided a pool of reservists. But more importantly, it promoted an image of the benefits of Empire.

The Welsh tribes did not have a tradition of living together in permanent groups or towns. Their own settlements were not really towns, since they had no administrative function. The Roman army in forts was an entirely new idea – and the Welsh, adaptable as always, gathered around them. The Welsh economy was still largely at a subsistence level and didn't produce enough surplus to support a warrior class who fought but were not productive. The Welsh chieftains had always maintained their power through territorial conflict since it was the easiest way to acquire more wealth. Now they had a different model.

AD 60 Menai Strait

The Anglesey Problem

Although the Romans took control of most of Wales, they still needed to deal with Anglesey. Not only did the island have a significant natural population, but also it served as a hiding place and sanctuary for dissidents. At least that is what some scholars believe. They were certainly seen as primitives who stood in the way of Roman dominance.

The Greek writer Strabo said of the Welsh: 'The whole race is madly fond of war, high-spirited and quick to battle, but otherwise straightforward and not of evil character.' (Strabo, *Historical Sketches*) Generous words, but the Welsh were up against a much more methodical and organised opposition. And the Romans were never keen to accommodate different points of view. For them, Ynys Mon was an irritation, a reservoir of rebellion which seemed to bring the Welsh together which then, as now, was no mean feat. Others are less convinced by the romantic image of a Welsh resistance and believe that the Romans were more motivated by a desire for possession of a prosperous island with good farmland and copper mines, forests and fishing, which could survive happily without mainland Wales.

It is clear that the defenders of Anglesey lacked the organisation and the training of the legions. They were brave and shouted vile abuse at the Romans as they approached. But it was a classic sticks and stones situation. Shout what you like, but the Romans had fought their way across Europe to get to Anglesey and had always put their faith in something a bit sharper than name-calling. General Gaius Suetonius Paulinus had brought catapults or *ballistae* to throw flaming missiles at least 600 yards, and *onagers* which threw boulders. So there was a tactic which we can all recognise – an advance on the enemy made beneath a bombardment. You can see how the Romans taught future military strategists a great deal.

They brought flat-bottomed boats with them, but they were not tethered together to form a bridge, since the tides were too tricky. The infantry paddled across. The cavalry advanced by fording or, in deeper water, by swimming beside their horses. This was the most vulnerable part of the assault and they sustained some casualties at this point. But once ashore, they were a much more formidable opposition.

AD 60 Anglesey

The Island They Invaded Twice

It could be that the Roman historian Tacitus exaggerated the threat posed by the Celts on Anglesey in order to make the Roman success even more impressive. There were certainly plenty of them, but their equipment and tactics hardly put them at the forefront of contemporary warfare. 'On the beach stood the adverse array, a serried mass of arms and men, with women flitting between the ranks. In the style of Furies, in robes of deathly black and with dishevelled hair, they brandished their torches; while a circle of Druids, lifting their hands to heaven and showering imprecations, struck the troops with such an awe at the extraordinary spectacle'. (Tacitus, *The Annals*)

While the Welsh considered themselves to be possessed by divine inspiration, this cut little ice with the Romans. They were seasoned, hard-bitten and probably cynical old campaigners. Their job was to slice up barbarians. So they got on with it. Another day, another *sesterce*. Tacitus wrote: 'Then, reassured by their general, and inciting each other never to flinch before a band of females and fanatics, they charged behind the standards, cut down all who met them, and enveloped the enemy in his own flames.' Unsophisticated, perhaps, but generally effective. Conflict resolution, the Roman way.

The next step was to install a garrison among the conquered population, and to demolish the groves consecrated to 'their savage cults, for they considered it a pious duty to slake the altars with captive blood and to consult their deities by means of human entrails' (Tacitus).

How true this business about human sacrifice is, no one has ever been quite sure. It could have been merely an attempt to demonise and discredit an enemy. The Romans themselves were vicious and merciless. They butchered the population. The battle is still remembered in local names – The Field of the Long Battle, The Hill of Graves.

It was a brutal defeat and even though Governor of Roman Britain, Paulinus, was forced to return to the mainland to deal with Boudicca, Anglesey was never the same again. When Agricola invaded again in AD 75, resistance was quickly overcome and the island was finally garrisoned.

+ Suppressing the Welsh was hard work. Agricola was not killed in battle. He died, according to the historian Tacitus, from fatigue.

+ The *mullus* (red mullet) was a popular Roman delicacy. The scales of the fish turn bright red when it dies out of water. As a result, *mullus* were sometimes allowed to die slowly at the table or in the sauce in which they were served.

+ *Garum* was the name of a sauce added to everything. It was prepared by allowing salted fish, in particular mackerel intestines, to sit in the sun for between two and three months so that the fish decomposed. The mess was then filtered. The liquid was *garum*, while the solids were known as the *alec* and used as a savoury spread. Because of the smell, the production of *garum* was banned within the confines of a city. Today, similar sauces are called *nam pla*.

+ It was the sign of a fine meal if it had been flavoured with spices to such an extent that a diner could not tell either by smell or taste what ingredients had been used in the production of a dish.

 AD 70 Caerleon

The Fountain with the Dolphin's Head

Caerleon was a very important site, with about 6,000 soldiers stationed there at one time. They called it Isca Silurum and it was one of the most important military sites in Europe. There had never been anything like the Roman army in Wales before; it was organised, trained and tactically aware. Their fortresses, like Caerleon, were symbols of their power and their intention to stay.

The Augustan legion, previously stationed in Exeter, were based here. They were known as 'Caracalla's Own', after the nickname of the Emperor Augustus who acquired it because he wore a hooded garment called a *caracalla*. It was a high-profile legion and emphasised the Roman determination to dominate and control Wales.

Gerald Cambrensis described Caerleon as an imposing ruin upon the landscape, and the ruins have always been a tourist attraction. Many artefacts were sold during the eighteenth and nineteenth centuries as tourist souvenirs and thus lost. Caerleon was an extensive fortress, with a large outdoor swimming pool which held 80,000 gallons of water. At the shallow end of the pool there was a fountain with a dolphin's head. There were kitchens – where pie dishes were found along with legionary workshops, barracks and communal latrines.

There was a large amphitheatre to provide entertainment at this extreme end of the Empire. It had separate entrances into the arena for animals and gladiators, with small chambers where they could wait their turn. There were cheap seats, a separate area for women and children and the Roman equivalent of executive boxes. The site of the amphitheatre was excavated by Sir Mortimer Wheeler in 1926 and it is strange but true that the site was purchased by the *Daily Mail* to facilitate the dig. They then presented the site to the nation.

The stone from the Roman fortifications was recycled locally to build houses. Of course, this happened everywhere once the Romans left.

+ A large number of carefully carved gemstones were found beneath the Caerleon baths. They had been dropped by bathers.

+ The use of coal as a fuel for the burning of lime and for heating is first seen at Caerleon.

+ A *Genius Paterfamilias* was found in Caerleon – a small model to act as a personal guardian and probably given to a soldier by his family: essentially, it was a good-luck charm.

+ The first Roman fort to be built in Wales was at Burrium (Usk) in about AD 55.

+ The Britannia As of AD 154 is a coin which is frequently found buried across Britain.

Memories of the Romans soon faded and for years local people believed that the remains of the fortress were in fact the remains of the court of King Arthur.

AD 78 Trawsfynydd

Tomen y Mur

This was a Roman fortress on Mynydd Maentwrog in Snowdonia; it was intended to protect the road to Segontium (Caernarfon) and to act as a reminder to any surviving Ordovices of the power of the Empire. It was built by Agricola in AD 78.

The fort was discovered when a large number of bricks appeared as a result of a farmer ploughing in the middle of the nineteenth century. He subsequently confessed to cutting through some defences when he was building gates to his farm. Other Roman bricks had been used to build retaining walls. The original Roman walls had been constructed with remarkable precision. The masons had not used cement and yet it is still impossible to slip a blade between the stones. Such craftsmanship suggests that they intended to stay at Tomen y Mur for quite a while.

The location was so remote that it is only one of two fortresses in Wales (the other being Moridunium – Carmarthen) that had its own amphitheatre to entertain the troops. Normally such places were reserved for towns like Caerleon. But this was probably not the most popular of postings, in a bleak, dangerous and lawless area.

For the people of Snowdonia of course historical concerns cut little ice. They had a life to lead, on top of and not around the ruins; for example, a tramway from the Braich Ddu slate quarry went straight through the site. Part of the site was used as a sheep dip.

There are also burial mounds for centurions who died such a long way from home. One such soldier was Julius Perpetius who, we are told on his tombstone, was responsible for building a twenty-pace length of wall. His gravestone, like others, had been used as part of the walls of Harlech Castle. One grave is particularly large and was built to form a pyramid with a flat top – certainly the grave of someone important. Urns have also been found with cremated remains in them, one containing the blade of a dagger (perhaps indicating a soldier) and another with a long bodkin, perhaps suggesting that this was a female.

- The Cohors Primae Cornoviorum was the only recorded native unit to have served in the Roman army in Britain. They were recruited from the Cornovii tribe.

- There is a fragment of a sandstone tombstone in the Brecknock Museum in Brecon which was found at the end of the nineteenth century. The poignant inscription reads: 'In memory of Candidus, son of … trooper in the Vettonian Spanish cavalry. Set up by his heirs … Clemens and Domitius.' Candidus lived for twenty years and served three.

- Soldiers were encouraged to save their pay and their savings were usually kept in the regimental safe. They were also encouraged to pay for their own funerals through an army fund.

- The fragment of a tombstone found in Usk indicates that it once marked the grave of a child of a Roman soldier.

 AD 100 Dolaucothi

The Gold Standard

The Dolaucothi Gold Mines are the reason why Roman chroniclers claimed that Britain was rich in gold and other precious metals. After all there was already a long tradition of mining in Wales even before they arrived. This was certainly part of their justification to mount an invasion across the Channel. The Romans soon established gold mines in two main locations, Dolaucothi and Dolgellau in North Wales.

Their mines were worked in part by convicts, who performed the intensive labour. They used simple machinery to crush the ore to extract the gold particles. They left the devices lying around when they departed, soon to be overgrown by the vegetation. It is certainly strange but true to realise that the knowledge that there was gold in the Carmarthen hills was subsequently lost. The Romans left no record of their mines and the workings were soon lost in the dense woodland for over 1,000 years until a geologist called Warington Smythe rediscovered them in 1844.

The mines go straight into the mountainside and the marks left by the Romans are still visible on the walls. They built huge reservoirs

- Roman travellers did not use maps for travelling; they were too inaccurate. Instead they used directions which listed the places to be found along the road and the distances between them.

- The Antonine Itinerary was a Roman travel guide. It identified Monmouth as being on Route 13.

- The penal system made prisoners repair roads as part of their punishment.

- Parts of Britain developed specialist products for export to the rest of the Roman Empire – like kitchenware from Dorset. This does not appear to have happened in Wales, which might mean that it was little more than frontier territory.

- In 1848 silver Roman coins were found in Abergavenny by a workman, but they disappeared after he exchanged them for 1s 6d and a pint of beer.

- Abergavenny was called Gobannium by the Romans. It probably derived its name from the Celtic word *gobann*, meaning ironsmith. Gefenni, the original name of the River Gavenny, means 'river of the ironsmith'. Of course, Abergavenny means mouth of the Gefenni.

- Romans developed their own central heating systems – a hypercaust. Heat from an outside furnace went into buildings under floors that were raised on pillars. The heat then went into rooms through vents.

- The Romans happily matched up their gods with local gods. In South Wales the god Ocelus was identified with Mars, the Roman god of war.

- In 1844, a Roman well was uncovered in Caernarfon. At the bottom was a collection of kitchenware, including deer antlers, a boar's tusk, oyster shells, pottery, a large key and an egg cup.

- A stone coffin was unearthed during the building of a new housing development in Undy, Monmouthshire. It was made in the third or fourth century and contained the skeleton of a woman in her twenties, 5ft 4in tall. She came from a wealthy family, since the coffin was made from specially imported and expensive Bath stone.

to wash the ore, which was transported from the River Cothi on an aqueduct carrying 2 million gallons a day. The miners extracted the ore by building a fire against the rocks, then placing the heated rock in a tank of cold water which would crack it, allowing the quartz to be removed. It was then crushed by water-powered machinery. It was washed again to separate out the gold, which would be trapped in a sheep's fleece at the bottom of the tanks. Then the fleece was burned, leaving the gold behind. It was quite a sophisticated operation.

They removed about half a million tons of rock in their time. Each ton produced a tiny amount of gold – perhaps the size of a sugar cube. In the end they extracted over half a ton of gold. This was smelted and then transported as ingots to mints throughout the Empire, and particularly to the mint at Lyon, in France.

AD 110 Chester

The Amphitheatre

Deva Victrix (Chester) was a really important settlement with a huge effect upon Wales, for it was the base for the troops who suppressed the north and Anglesey. The purpose of the fortifications was to maintain control over North Wales – it was on Watling Street, where it intersected with a number of other major roads. It was a large fortress and sustained an extensive population. There were all the facilities and developments you would normally associate with a Roman town, including an impressive amphitheatre, which had all the attractions and facilities of a modern sports stadium. It was initially built out of wood but an improved and more permanent stone structure soon replaced it. There were separate entrances to allow easy access to the different seating areas, for the structure could accommodate 8,000 spectators. There were also executive boxes for the privileged. Excavations into the seating area uncovered animal bones, which indicated that tradesmen circulated amongst the crowds, selling chicken

legs and beef ribs; a crowd of this size was not one to be ignored. Bowls decorated with gladiatorial scenes have been found too, which seem to have been sold as souvenirs. Crowds would have thrilled to wrestling, boxing, cock fighting, hunting wild animals and gladiatorial bouts, which were later brought together to create the game of rugby.

After the entertainment the sand on the arena floor was raked over and soiled parts dumped outside the walls. This sand was often stained with blood and investigations have uncovered a human tooth hidden within it.

As a large and managed area it was also very convenient for weapons training and military parades and other communal events like public executions. An arena like this was an essential part of the Roman identity. It was something that defined them and represented civilization in a remote and sometimes hostile area.

> ✦ Gladiatorial contests produced fierce rivalries with visiting
> fans. On one occasion there was name-calling in Pompeii at
> the arena, which led to the drawing of swords. Some spectators
> were killed and Pompeii was banned from holding further
> contests for ten years.

After the Romans left, the amphitheatre was still used, though for residential purposes. Cesspits were dug by the Saxons and slowly the amphitheatre slipped from view. It was eventually rediscovered in 1929.

 AD 150 Bath

Defixio

The Romans imported some new habits to Wales, obviously the sort of things that the innocent Welsh had never previously considered. Like curses. They would, in times of stress, scratch out messages wishing ill health (or worse) upon those who had upset them. This was a curse tablet, or *defixio*. One was found buried in the arena in Caerleon and it was written by a gladiator asking for the help of Nemesis, the goddess of fate and vengeance. He had had clothes stolen and so he retrospectively donated them to Nemesis in the hope that she would go and get them back for him. The translation given by the British Museum reads: 'I give you this cloak and these boots. Let no man take them except at the peril of his life.' (It seems a bit of a long shot to me but these were desperate times, especially when your clothes disappeared.)

Defixii were often rolled up and hidden under floors or in walls or wells, to secretly spread their mystic poison. Sometimes they were accompanied by a small doll or figure pierced by nails. In the British Museum there is a fine example from Moorgate in London, scratched on a small piece of lead: 'I curse Tretia Maria and her life and mind and memory and liver and lungs mixed up together, and her words, thoughts and memory; thus may she be unable to speak what things are concealed, nor be able …' Poor Tretia Maria. The lead had been punctured by seven holes designed to increase the effectiveness of the spell. Obviously she upset someone. And however vicious it all appears, you do wonder what else she wouldn't be able to do.

One example from Maidstone has fourteen names on it; a rather scattergun approach to revenge, in my view. But it wasn't uncommon, especially with the theft of clothes from the public baths. Helping yourself to someone else's tunic from the storage lockers was regarded as the lowest form of behaviour. Some bathers hired slaves (*capsarii*) to watch their belongings in the *apodyterium*, but all too often they fell asleep. This is why baths were full of *defixii*. One hundred and thirty of them have been found at Bath.

And I am sorry to have to tell you that many of the names of the accused appear to be Welsh.

AD 300 Whitchurch

Medical Negligence

Whitchurch is currently in Shropshire, though it was regarded by the Romans as being in Wales, which is why it sneaks into this book. That and the fact that it is such a good story.

During the excavations of a Roman villa, a skeleton was found buried beneath the floor. It was a male body, probably in its mid-twenties, and in the skull there was a circular hole just above the right ear. This was the mark of surgery – a trepanning had taken place. This was the removal of a circular piece of bone from the head, generally to release pressure in the skull or to release evil spirits. It was a procedure which was practised in many different places across the ancient world, from Asia to Central America, from Egypt to – it seems – Whitchurch. It is the earliest known surgical procedure, with evidence found even in Neolithic skulls.

On this occasion the piece of bone removed had been replaced before burial and was found lying inside the skull. Often it was kept and worn as a charm to keep away evil spirits.

Now the implication that will delight all you cold-case fans is that something dodgy was going on here. It was, after all, illegal to bury a body inside the walls of a settlement. So perhaps the patient died on the operating table and the surgeon tried to cover his tracks by burying the body where he stood. Pretty desperate you might think, but clearly he got away with it since the body was still there. And there was a Roman cemetery outside Whitchurch, so Dr Death had no reason at all to dig up the floor – unless there was something to hide.

The unfortunate patient was about 5ft tall but it seems that his upper right wisdom tooth was badly decayed. This would have been extremely painful and might have been the reason why he'd taken the fatal step of seeking medical advice. Sometimes desperate pain breeds desperate measures. To be honest, if I ever go to the dentist and he starts grinning wildly and plans to drill into my head, then I might decide to go private.

> + A significant number of the bodies found in the Roman cemetery at Cirencester were suffering from gout.

 ## AD 386 Edinburgh

Cunedda the Good Hound

Cunedda. The greatest of all the early Welsh heroes. And he came from Scotland. Yes indeed. Oh, and his name means 'good hound'. Strange but true.

Basically he was invited down from Scotland by either the Romans or, more probably, by the British king Vortigern. He was promised land, if only he would keep the Irish at bay. And that

is what he did. In so doing he established the kingdom of Gwynedd, which in turn established a dynasty which ruled Wales for generations. He was born in around AD 386 and his arrival in the fifth century is considered to be the beginning of the history of modern Wales. Throughout the rest of Welsh history, everyone tried to authenticate their rule by claiming direct descent from him.

+ St Germanus of Auxerre had an unusual approach to military strategy. On a visit to Wales in AD 429 he led the natives to a famous victory over Saxon invaders at Garmon's Field outside Mold. As the enemy approached he hid his forces and made them shout out 'Alleluiah!' very loudly three times. It was so loud that the Saxons were convinced that they were outnumbered. They turned and ran and were cut down by the pursuing Welsh warriors.

+ There was a significant change in the climate in the third century, with lower temperatures and higher rainfall. Then, from the seventh century, there was an improvement until conditions were similar to those of today. Temperatures continued to rise until AD 1000.

+ It adds to your sense of confusion – I know that it does – but you do need to know where the terms Wales and Cymru came from. During the Dark Ages, Wales was that bit of the country to the west of the land that could be easily cultivated and was therefore worth having. The indigenous population – the Celts and the Romano-British – had been pushed in that direction by the invading Saxons, who called them *walha*, which meant foreigner or stranger. They called themselves *brythoniad*, or Britons, because they had once inhabited most of the mainland.

As time went on, they started to call themselves *y cymry*, which meant 'fellow countrymen'. In this way they established a sense of identity in the face of the invaders who had usurped their lands and called *them* 'strangers'. The first recorded use of the term *cymry* comes from the seventh century in a poem called 'In Praise of Cadwallon'.

He became King of Gwynedd during the early fifth century and created a stability which allowed the development of Wales as a separate entity. He was celebrated for his strength and his courage, and as a leader commanded devotion and respect. He appears to have come from Manaw Gododdin, the region around Edinburgh in south-east Scotland. He was called Cunedda ap Edern. His grandfather was possibly a Romano-British official called 'Paternus of the Scarlet Robe' who, in addition to having a fantastic name, had kept the Picts in their place. Suppression – the family franchise. Exported to Wales in the disintegration of the Roman Empire he was the right man at the right time.

Essentially, Cunedda was hired muscle. It is often the case that once you have hired them you can't get rid of them – and this was certainly true of Cunedda. He had eight sons, amongst whom the lands of Wales were divided. After all, Cunedda seems to have controlled all the land between the Dee and the Teifi.

The hill of Allt Cunedda at Kidwelly in Carmarthenshire is associated with him, and it is believed by some to be his burial place. The hill was excavated in the nineteenth century and well-preserved skeletons were recovered, including one which was found in a seated position. Sadly these precious items disappeared forever when they were sent to various museums for safe keeping.

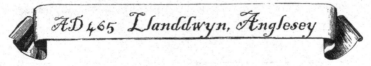

AD 465 Llanddwyn, Anglesey

Ice Maiden

St Dwynwen is Wales' very own patron saint of lovers and her day is 25 January. She is also the patron saint of sick animals but let's put that to one side for a moment.

As you might have guessed, she was the prettiest of Brychan Brycheinog's twenty-four daughters – no mean achievement, given the competition. She fell in love with a prince called Maelon Dafodrill, an unfortunate name, which perhaps put her father off. He decided he would offer her in marriage to another.

There are different variants of the tale – in one Maelon presses his attentions upon her far too vigorously, pre-empting their marriage. But whatever happened, the consequences remain the same. Dwynwen was very upset and begged God to intercede and help her forget him. For his part, he sent one of his top angels, who appeared before her with a magic potion. However, it was Maelon who drank it and was turned unexpectedly into a block of ice.

Dwynwen was then given three wishes. Her first was that Maelon should be thawed. The second wish was that God should fulfil the hopes and dreams of true lovers and the third was that she should never marry. Perhaps a man who had so recently defrosted was not an attractive proposition. All three wishes were granted and in thanks, Dwynwen became a nun. She founded a convent on the island of Llanddwyn off the coast of Anglesey and the ruins can still be seen. A holy well was named after her and it became a place of pilgrimage after her death in AD 465. The faithful believed that the fish and eels that lived in the well could predict the success of any relationship.

Apparently.

+ Brychan, the King of Brycheiniog, lived at Talgarth in the fifth century AD. He had three wives, twenty-four daughters and twenty-two sons and probably a personal secretary to keep track of all the birthdays. Given the numbers involved, it is hardly surprising that almost all of the saints of South Wales are allegedly descended from him.

+ Llantwit Major was the site of a Celtic monastery founded by St Illtud from Brittany. Twit is an Irish form of St Illtud's name.

+ There is an old Welsh tradition which claims that St Patrick was the son of Mawon, from Gower.

 AD 547 Rhos

An Attack of the Vapours

He was known as Maelgwn Hir – Maelgwn the Tall – and he was King of Gwynedd in the sixth century. He was true leader of men, a Christian ruler, founding churches everywhere, perhaps even founding Bangor – and regarded by history as a bit of a villain.

Maelgwn was the great-grandson of Cunedda and continued the expulsion of the Irish settlers from Anglesey and North Wales. His position as King of Gwynedd appears to have given him some superiority over the other local kings. He died in AD 547, in what was known as 'a great mortality' or the 'Yellow Plague' of Rhos, where he was buried. It was believed that it was caused by vapours arising from the carcasses of the dead.

Maelgwn's great claim to fame is that he usurped power from his uncle, lived for a while as a monk, then gave that up, married, divorced, killed his nephew and married his widow. He might have killed his own wife too, though that isn't clear. Some records also suggest that he combined all this with an 'addiction to sodomy', though that might just be gossip. But overall I think you can see that he carried with him a number of unresolved issues.

There is a windmill named after him on Anglesey.

+ Amusements in Wales at this time included throwing an iron bar, throwing a large stone, running, swimming, archery and throwing the javelin. Less manly pursuits included hunting, fishing and bird catching.

 AD 560 *Llanddewi Brefi*

St David

Many of the stories of his life are strange, but whether they are true is quite another matter. St David has, though, become the enduring symbol of Wales and Welshness.

His best known miracle is said to have happened whilst preaching in the middle of a large crowd at the Synod of Brefi. The ground where he stood is said to have risen up to form a small hill to enable full congregational involvement. A white dove, apparently less incontinent that its descendants, settled on his shoulder and became his emblem.

You can understand his need to be seen – but did West Wales need another hill? It is certainly the only mound in the village. He was a teacher and preacher, dedicated to the promotion of the Christian faith. He came from an aristocratic family. His mother was St Non, and clearly a role model; he established monasteries and churches and collected followers.

His monastic rules were rather severe. Monks had to pull the plough themselves; animals not allowed. They could drink only water and eat only bread with salt and herbs, which is not the kind of balanced diet contemporary nutrition would support. Evenings should be spent in prayer and reading. No personal possessions were allowed at all.

He promoted the virtues of a simple life, urging his followers to refuse to eat meat or drink beer. On a personal level he liked nothing better than standing up to his neck in a cold lake, contemplating. It doesn't appear to have done him any harm though, since he apparently lived until he was 100. He died on Tuesday, 1 March AD 590 and his body is buried in St David's Cathedral in Pembrokeshire.

Oddly he is associated with the idea of corpse candles: lights which indicate an imminent death. He prayed for something that would warn people of their demise so that they could prepare themselves for the inevitable. Corpse candles is what he got, which travelled just above the ground between the cemetery and the seriously unwell. I suppose in these circumstances you have to take what you are given.

+ St Teilo (possibly) founded a monastery in Llandeilo and was probably the third Bishop of St David's. It is said that his skull became the property of a family in Llandeilo. Even into the nineteenth century they apparently offered visitors the chance to drink water from the skull in order for them to benefit from its curative powers.

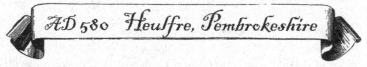

AD 580 Heulfre, Pembrokeshire

Stone Ground

This is built into a wall between Maes y Garreg farm and Heulfre in Pembrokeshire. It is an early Christian stone, which has on it a cross within a circle. It is called the Mesur y Dorth stone, which means 'measure of bread'. St David established a custom that when times were hard, the size of a loaf of bread should be controlled. Consequently the Bishop of St David's ordered that the size of a loaf of bread should be equal to the size of the circle on the Mesur y Dorth stone. It is also said that pilgrims on their way to St David's would stop off at the stone to eat their last meal before pressing on to their destination.

The stone is 1m high and is actually in the village of Croes-goch – Red Cross. This reflects the story that there was once a battle there which resulted in such slaughter that a river of blood sprang forth, forming itself into the image of a cross.

There is a megalithic standing stone in the churchyard at Cilgerren, upon which Ogham script was carved. There are short and long notches along the edge, a form of writing used by the Irish and dating back to the sixth century. They were often erected over the graves of chieftains. This one says 'Here lies Trenegussus, son of Macutrenus'.

+ Abbot Armel from south-east Wales died in about AD 570. Prayers to him were said to cure headaches, fever, colic, gout and rheumatism.

+ The name of the Carmarthenshire village Pumpsaint comes from a Carmarthen legend of five saintly brothers – Gwyn, Gwynio, Celynin, Gwynaro and Ceitho – who left the imprints of their heads on a large stone they sheltered against during a violent storm (*pump* means five). The storm had been created by a sorcerer who was trying to lure them to his cave.

 AD 613 Heronbridge

The Slaughter of the Saints

This was not the most glorious engagement in Welsh military history. It was a major victory for the army of Aethelfrith of Northumberland over a Welsh army drawn from Powys and Gwynedd. The reasons for the invasion are unclear – perhaps he was in pursuit of a rival Edwin, who was in exile in Gwynedd. No one can be sure.

The site of the battle is also unclear. Some have suggested Perlan Fangor (Bangor orchard), though it is more likely to have been at Heronbridge near Chester. Excavations there have uncovered a mass burial site. They were all male skeletons with fatal head injuries, entirely consistent with the nature of a brutal encounter in which so many Welsh leaders were killed. They had been buried carefully and respectfully, which suggests they were Northumberland soldiers, rather than the defeated Welsh.

A large number of monks had walked up from their monastery in Bangor-on-Dee to watch the battle, support the home team and celebrate an inevitable triumph. It wasn't wise. They gathered together and prayed loudly for a Welsh victory before battle commenced. Aethelfrith was not impressed. He is reputed to have said, 'If then they cry to their God against us, in truth though they do not bear arms, yet they fight against us, because they oppose us by their prayers'. So he ordered his army to kill them. It became known as 'The Slaughter of the Saints'.

Now, Aethelfrith was a pagan. He was not converted to Christianity until after his death, so he might well have objected to the praying monks, though it is more likely to have been a tactic to unbalance and disrupt the Welsh army, who would have tried to defend them. He was, after all, known as 'Flesaur' – 'the twister'. His tactic worked. Anywhere between 200 and 1,200 monks were killed in a nasty hors d'oeuvre before the main event. Only a handful escaped.

Then he turned his attentions to the Welsh. It was a crushing defeat.

 AD 660 Clynnog Fawr

The Primal Cow

It is certainly true that Beuno has more churches dedicated to him than anyone else in North Wales, which must mean something.

The fact that he is the patron saint of sick children and diseased cattle is obviously something to be proud of, but hardly explains his popularity.

The story is that he was sent from Powys on missionary work in north-east Wales, a thankless task, even then. He heard a man shouting to his dog in English and was so shocked that he decided to move further west until he was out of reach of English voices. He said to his monks, 'Let us leave this place for the nation of this man. He has a strange language which is abominable and I heard his voice'. (S. Baring-Gold, *Lives of the British Saints*, 1907) We should be grateful that he was spared the thrill of a visit to Paddington.

But perhaps his popularity is explained by the fact that he seems to have become associated with much older beliefs. His grave was venerated for centuries at Clynnog Fawr on the Llyn Peninsula in Caernarfonshire. It always offered cures for epilepsy, rickets and impotence – as long as you slept on it. Naturally there was a waiting list. When it was excavated in 1914, it is said that inside the pelvis of the skeleton were the bones of a child, which to be honest does ask rather more questions than it answers.

Certainly a strange mixture of beliefs surrounded him. At the church in Clynnog Fawr there was a custom which survived until at least the eighteenth century that bulls should be sacrificed there: half for God and half for Beuno. This is either a folk memory of the ancient Celtic creation myth of the 'Primal Cow' from which all life originated, or it reflects the conviction that St Beuno had an early family sized chest freezer.

He was a man of many gifts. He once arranged for savage beasts to tear apart a man who was following him, only to discover that it was his servant. So Beuno reassembled the body parts, all except a missing eyebrow which might have been eaten, and the servant was restored to life. His party trick was to bring back to life decapitated victims, which he did on four or five occasions.

St Beuno? He was always keen to stay ahead.

✦ Issui, a holy man at Patrishow near Abergavenny, was murdered by an ungrateful traveller to whom he had given shelter, who then threw his body down a well. As a result the water in the well displayed curative powers. A French visitor apparently 'washed away his leprosy' at St Issui's Well at some point in the eleventh century. The visitor was so pleased that he paid for a church to be built on the site.

 ## AD 682 Heaven

The Leek

The leek is the vegetable widely recognised as the national symbol of Wales. It is a long-established tradition. Welsh archers at the Battle of Crécy wore the green and white colours of the leek. Shakespeare refers to them in *Henry V* when the king tells Fluellen that he is wearing a leek since, 'I am Welsh, you know, good countryman.' (*Henry V*, Act 4, Scene 7)

The household accounts of the Tudor kings record expenditure on leeks to be worn by household guards on St David's Day. Today on St David's Day every soldier in a Welsh regiment will wear one – and then often eat it raw if he believes it will upset his mates in the barracks.

The key to it all is allegedly revealed by the Elizabethan poet Michael Drayton, who tells the story that King Cadwaladr of Gwynedd ordered his soldiers to wear a leek in their caps to identify themselves in battle against the hated Saxons. This was in a time before uniforms – and in a time when battles were scheduled to be fought in fields of leeks. Poor Cadwaladr. He might have been King of Gwynedd, but it didn't stop him dying of the plague in AD 682.

But it would seem that the Welsh association with the leek is very deep rooted – unlike the leek itself. St David used the short roots to symbolise the simple material needs of the true Christian who, like the leek, should put his energies into reaching up towards heaven.

It was always regarded as an important remedy. It could cure the common cold, deter evil spirits, relieve the pain of childbirth, protect against wounds in battle and protect you against lightning strikes.

Scoff if you will, but I like leeks and eat them as often as I can and I have never been struck by lightning. Proof indeed. I cannot, however, verify claims that if you sleep with a leek beneath your pillow you will dream of your future husband.

Some might say that the daffodil is the preferred symbol of Welsh identity – but remember that one of the Welsh names for the flower is *cenhinen Bedr*, which means Peter's leek.

 AD 785 Prestatyn

Offa's Dyke

Offa's Dyke was a huge undertaking, one of the great achievements: an earthwork running very roughly along the border between England and Wales. A unique and linear ancient monument – and one that you are allowed to walk along.

Parts of it have now disappeared but you can still enjoy the long-distance footpath that links north and south through an area of particular beauty, linking Prestatyn and Sedbury, near Chepstow.

Construction is believed to have started in AD 785 and, given its scale, obviously continued for quite a while. The reasons why it was built remain unclear, but we do know that it was commissioned by Offa, the King of Mercia who has an additional and significant claim to fame in that he established the penny as the basic monetary unit.

The dyke was intended to mark the boundary between Mercia and Powys, to keep the Welsh out (or indeed the English, depending on your perspective). What it achieved more than anything else was that it offered a clear definition of what Wales actually was.

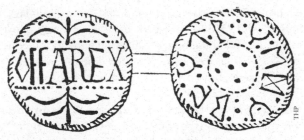

231.—Silver **Penny of Offa, King of Mercia.**

Originally it was over 20m wide and 8 high – and of course 270 km long. It was never really much of a fortification. It was never enough to delay a rabid attacker in whichever direction they were heading. It was more of a show of power, with the spoil piled carefully on the Mercian side for extra height. They had an extended observation platform. The Welsh had a ditch.

It is likely that different communities along the length of it were obliged to build a particular section. There may in fact have been a similar structure in place before Offa. There is some archaeological evidence from carbon dating that suggests some of the earthworks date from 300 years before Offa.

The writer George Borrow, always rather fanciful, said that it was the custom for the English to cut off the ears of every Welshman found to the east of the dyke and for the Welsh to hang every Englishman to the west, but in reality this would have proved to be a serious inconvenience to all those who tried to trade along the border. And as we all know, in the end it is economics that matters.

✦ According to the Mabinogion, Math the King of Gwynedd
had to rest with his feet in the lap of a virgin, except in
time of war. When his nephews raped the king's footholder,
Goewin, he punished them severely. Well you would.

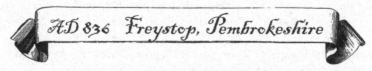

AD 836   Freystop, Pembrokeshire

Hairy Trousers

Regner Lodbrog was the celebrated and semi-legendary King of Denmark who left his own mark on Wales. He was a fearsome warrior who liked nothing better than laying waste to someone else's country. He ended his days being bitten to death by serpents in a pit into which he was thrown by Ella, the King of Northumberland. These were exciting times.

Regner appears to have toured around Wales in the ninth century, spreading destruction and ruin wherever he went. He enjoyed a bit of mayhem, which did not endear him to local residents. There was an especially bloody encounter at Burry

Holms on the Gower coast and another at Freystrop near Milford Haven in around AD 836. In his poem 'The Dying Ode of Regner Lodbrog', allegedly written by his personal poet, he describes the battles in Wales: 'The blue steel all reeking with blood fell at length upon the golden mail. Many a virgin bewailed the laughter of that morning', which is as about as close as you will ever get to seeing his compassionate side.

The poem ends with: 'My hours of my life are past away. I die laughing.'

It is good to preserve a positive outlook, even if you are at the bottom of a pit of vipers.

Lodbrog means 'hairy trousers', in case you were wondering.

+ Three Viking ships landed at Burry Holms in order to burn the church and slaughter the people of Llangennith. Whilst they were busy the men from Rhossili set fire to their ships. A cunning move. But was it wise to stop them leaving?

+ Viking influence is seen in the names that survive for places along the British coast – Stackpole Head, Skokholm Island, the Naze, Strumble Head. Lundy comes from the Norse for puffin – *lundi*. Swansea may be a corruption of the Norse Sweyn's Ey, meaning Sweyn's Island, after Sweyn Forkbeard who may have been shipwrecked there. Vikings didn't really penetrate far inland in Wales, generally preferring a quick getaway. And they didn't stay around long in the way that they did in the North of England.

+ The waterway at Milford Haven was used by Vikings as a place to shelter. In AD 878 the Viking warlord Hubba, brother to Ivar the Boneless, over-wintered there with twenty-three ships, giving his name to the area of Hubberston.

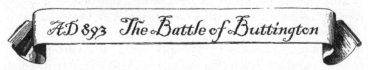

AD 893 The Battle of Buttington

Pain Relief

This was a very significant encounter, which has now been almost entirely forgotten. And it was notable too, for the Welsh and the

Alfred the Great.

English fought together to defeat the Danes. Unusual certainly, and perhaps strange. But true.

The Danes had by all accounts been having a hard time of things on the Continent and so turned their attentions to King Alfred's kingdom where victory – and life – might be a little easier. They moved away from their base in East Anglia and Northumberland and ravaged most of central England. When they reached the Severn they marched to the north. It is probably what Danes were programmed to do.

An English force was recruited from the towns in the west of England, who were joined by Welsh soldiers, their own differences forgotten for a while in the face of a common enemy. Led by Aethelred, Lord of the Mercians, they followed the Danes and attacked them from the rear at Buttington, near Welshpool. They then besieged the invaders, who hastily erected earthworks. Trapped, they were reduced to eating their own horses. When they tried to break out they came up against a well-fed, well-organised and motivated opposition. Trapped against the river, with the Welsh on the other bank, they sustained heavy losses and fled back to East Anglia.

Burial pits were uncovered in Buttington, full of skulls and assorted bones. Teeth from the skulls were sold by local workmen as a remedy against toothache. After all, the teeth had not given their owners any problems for hundreds of years.

It was sadly a temporary triumph. The Danes regrouped and marched on Chester. The English army destroyed all sources of food that could sustain the Danes, but they merely moved into Wales for their supplies, thus devastating large parts of Gwent and Brycheiniog and effectively ending any lasting co-operation between the English and the understandably resentful Welsh.

> ✦ In 901, as part of his rent on an estate, the Bishop of
> Winchester had to pay the king '12 sesters of sweet Welsh ale'.
> (Ian Spencer Hornsey, *A History of Beer and Brewing*, 2003)

AD 950 Seisyllwg

Hywel Dda

Hywel Dda (or Hywel the Good) was perhaps the greatest of the earliest rulers of Wales. The laws he established in the middle of the tenth century had more effect on Wales than those of anyone else.

He was a descendant of Rhodri Mawr, who had united the country to confront intruders like the Saxons and the Vikings. On his death the country was divided between his six sons and in such a divided situation there was weakness. Hywel was King of Seisyllwg (today Ceredigion and Carmarthen), but he soon acquired other regions.

The legal code which carries his name is now regarded as bringing justice and compassion and as being strangely enlightened:

+ Marriage was simply an agreement and divorce was permitted by common consent
+ In any claim of rape, precedence was always given to the woman's claims
+ There was no punishment for theft if it was the theft of food required to stay alive
+ Compensation for a victim was much more important than any punishment
+ Illegitimate children had the same rights as legitimate ones

How much he himself was responsible for remains unclear. Many of the laws which are ascribed to him predate his rule and there is a case to be made that he merely codified traditional Welsh law. It did not take its shape and priorities only from royal edicts. In fact, the earliest manuscripts outlining the code date from the thirteenth century, so we can only have the faintest idea of what tenth-century law was like.

But history has always regarded him as an intelligent and enlightened man. Even though he died in AD 950 he had a significant influence on the country, for his laws were enforced in Wales for almost 600 years – until Henry VIII passed the Act of Union in 1536.

In about AD 958 Edgar, the English king, demanded his annual tribute from the Welsh of 300 wolves' heads, which was apparently paid for a total of 540 years.

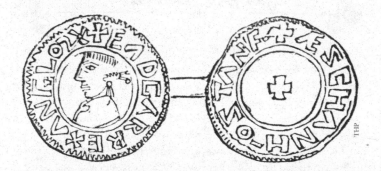

241.—Silver Penny of Eadgar, King of England.

✦ It was quite common in West Wales for women to attempt to predict the future using the blade bone of a ram. The right shoulder blade was best, obviously, and it had to have been stripped of any flesh. It mustn't be roasted, merely boiled until it was bare. Only then did it possess wonderful properties. As Geraldus Cambrensis commented in his *Cambriae Descriptio*, with it they could predict future events, reveal hidden mysteries or discover what was happening far away: 'They declare, also, by means of signs, the undoubted symptoms of approaching peace and war, murders and fires, domestic adulteries, the state of the king, his life and death.' A low-tech version of the internet, I suppose.

It was easy to use too, though perhaps a little more challenging in its interpretation. The bone would be thrust into the fire and then the burned parts were knocked off and the remainder studied closely for clues.

I am still not convinced that it would be a reliable way of predicting lottery numbers, no matter how accurate it was in predicting world peace.

 1063 *Snowdonia*

Keeping Ahead of the King

The first Gruffydd ap Llewellyn – who dominated Welsh politics throughout the middle part of the eleventh century – does his best to sneak into Shakespeare, by association anyway.

He was a great-great-grandson of Hywel Dda and was probably born in 1007 into the Royal House of Gwynedd, though he was forced into exile by his cousin Iago ap Idwal who then became king. Gruffydd then found ambition and he began his ascent to power (after the murder of Iago, of course). First the north and then, after military campaigns, the south too was his. By 1055 he was the first – and last – to reign as an independent king over the whole of Wales.

He was the committed enemy of Harold Godwinson and Edward the Confessor and in 1055 he defeated the Earl of Hereford,

the wonderfully named Ralph the Timid, in battle. This provoked a response from the English and Gruffydd was outmanoeuvred. He went into hiding in Snowdonia where, in 1063, he was killed by his own household, the fatal blow delivered by Cynan ap Iago, the son of the first victim in Gruffydd's pursuit of power. The blood feud has always been a driving force in much of Welsh history.

Gruffydd's head was cut off and sent to Edward. Harold Godwinson received a more interesting prize, though: he married Gruffydd's widow, Ealdgyth (the granddaughter of Lady Godiva, in case you are interested). Three years later Ealdgyth was widowed once again at the Battle of Hastings.

The Welsh managed to kill the man who had held them together. As a result Wales was then divided into its traditional kingdoms so that the Norman invaders never had to face a unified opposition and it remained that way for almost 400 years.

It has been claimed that the House of Stuart was descended from Walter Fitzalan, the first High Steward of Scotland, and he was believed to have been the grandson of Fleance (Banquo's son in *Macbeth*) and Gruffydd ap Llewellyn's daughter, the child conceived whilst the young man was in exile briefly in Wales. Interestingly, this would mean that the Stuart dynasty had an entirely fictional ancestor. Fleance was invented.

> + Gruffydd ap Llewellyn once heard that a young man had
> enjoyed graphic erotic dreams about his beautiful young
> wife Ealdgyth. It was believed that dreams were the window
> into another reality, and you might think that the young man
> would have been advised to keep his mouth shut. The king
> was enraged and the dreamer was seized to be tortured and
> executed. The local Druid, however, found an admirable
> solution. The young man's family brought a herd of oxen to
> the banks of a river and Gruffydd accepted in recompense the
> reflections of the cattle that shimmered on the surface of the
> water. Virtual compensation for a virtual crime.

The first to take what's not his own
Would be the first to win a throne

– Welsh proverb

1108 Flanders

Say Hello to the Lettuce

A large number of people from Flanders settled in Wales at different times during the Middle Ages. Geraldus Cambrensis tells us that 'Henry I transported thither [into Pembrokeshire] all the Flemings then resident in England'. A large number had arrived following a catastrophic sea water flood in the Low Countries, which destroyed sand hills and embankments. The Elizabethan Welsh historian David Powel, in his book *The Historie of Cambria, now called Wales* (1584) tells us that: 'The yeare 1108 the rage of the sea did overflow and drowne a great part of the lowe countries of Flanders.' They originally settled in Cumberland.

It was a tradition to use Flemish mercenaries and builders. A number had originally accompanied William the Conqueror, and King Stephen had hired a significant number. But generally mercenaries were people you didn't want hanging around with time on their hands. So they were resettled in Wales.

Contemporary sources suggest that 'The realm of England was sore pestered with them whereupon King Henry devised to place them in Pembrokeshire' (*Holinshed's Chronicles*) hoping apparently that this would keep the Welsh in order. Certainly there was considerable antipathy between the Welsh and the Flemings. Intermarriage was virtually unknown. They 'differed from the Welshmen in tongue and manners'. There was soon a linguistic division that stretched across Pembrokeshire that neither side was happy to cross.

Geraldus Cambrensis described them as 'brave and robust, ever hostile to the Welsh.' They brought with them the tradition for woollen manufacture that the Welsh would adopt themselves and settled initially around The Hundred of Roose (Rhos) and Castlemartin. Tancred built the castle at Haverfordwest, Wizo established Wiston and Letard Litelking established Letterston.

They did not come empty-handed, either. They brought with them the tulip and introduced the cabbage, the lettuce and the gooseberry to Wales, thus transforming Welsh cuisine, to the considerable gratitude of the locals I am sure.

+ According to Geraldus Cambrensis, the Welsh took no interest in commerce, shipping and manufactures.

+ The diet of peasants at this time was usually a stew of cereals and vegetables, cooked with old bones.

1109 Cilgerran

Owain ap Cadwgan and his Anger Management Issues

Owain ap Cadwgan was part of a long tradition of adolescent males addicted to adrenalin – Vikings, Indian braves, Mods and Rockers. Irresponsible, uncontrolled, indiscriminate. He was a leader of what became known as *ynfydyon* – aggressive young men with swords and ego and a misplaced belief in their own immortality.

He was probably born in 1080. His hobbies included violence, abduction and pillage. He first appears in the historical record in 1106 when he killed two princes, Meurig and Griffri. In charity you might describe him as 'an interesting character', but you wouldn't have wanted to meet him in the woods. He was generally a dangerous killer.

Owain lived in uncertain times. His father, Cadwgan ap Bleddyn, ruled Powys and was involved in skirmishes and conflict with the Normans. In 1109, Cadwgan held a Christmas feast for all the rulers of Wales. During the banquet Owain heard stories of a beautiful Welsh noblewoman called Nest, married to Gerald of Windsor. She was also the mistress of King Henry, by whom she had had a son. This was clearly an affront to his national pride. Owain took a force of *ynfydyon* to Cilgerran near Cardigan where Gerald and Nest were staying. They burrowed underneath the gate, abducted Nest and her children and set fire to the castle. Her husband, Gerald, fled by sliding down the toilet.

Owain was outlawed and fled to Ireland but soon returned to rampage across West Wales, selling any captives into slavery. Owain fathered two sons with Nest – Llywelyn and Einion – before she was returned to her husband.

The situation changed in 1111 when Cadwgan was murdered. Henry granted Owain the Kingdom of Powys and efforts were made to rehabilitate him. He was knighted and taken on an expedition to Normandy, although he still found time to capture and blind his father's murderer, Madog ap Rhiryd, in 1113.

But there remained one unresolved issue. In 1115, when he was putting down an uprising in Carmarthen, Owain was ambushed and killed by Gerald of Windsor.

1170 *Alabama*

Madog – Once Upon a Time in the West

Some people think this is true.

Madog ab Owain Gwynedd, a twelfth-century prince from Gwynedd, sailed west from Llandrillo. His eight ships, led by *Gwennan Gorn*, landed at Mobile Bay, Alabama in 1170, over 300 years before Columbus. Madog then returned to Wales for additional settlers and they sailed away from Lundy Island in 1171, never to be seen again.

There is no proof that he landed in America, though plenty of circumstantial evidence eagerly seized upon by believers. The Welsh tradition is that they settled in the Mississippi Valley. They showed the Native Americans how to build stone forts, structures which few tribes used. It is claimed that Roman coins were found in them.

They moved northward through Alabama and then west, where through intermarriage, they became the light-skinned, bearded Mandan Indians of North Dakota. They used a small round boat made of buffalo hides (the bull boat) stretched over a willow frame, almost identical to the Welsh coracle. They had Welsh-style box-beds with curtains around them.

The search to find a Welsh-speaking tribe became an obsession for some. More than thirteen tribes at some point were identified as Welsh speaking before the Mandans were selected, because of a unique language and culture. Their mythology has been minutely analysed for evidence to support their Welsh origins. Other tribes have been scrutinised for their Irish and Portuguese origins too.

The belief in the Welsh settlement was promoted in Elizabethan times for political reasons. Madog was the means by which Queen Elizabeth could claim America as her legal possession, since he'd got there first. It was said that Columbus himself believed that the natives honoured the memory of a white man called Matec and that he wrote on his chart, 'these are Welsh waters'.

But just to confuse things slightly, there are those who are convinced all this is wrong. In fact it is Madoc ap Meurig who is our man, not Madog ap Owain Gwynedd, and he landed in Tennessee in about AD 560.

There is still work to be done, I think.

1175 Abergavenny

The Abergavenny Massacre

It was 1175 and it was time for a dinner party – and not any old dinner party either. At this one there would be no time for polite conversation, and only one dish would be served. That dish was revenge.

Henry Fitzmiles was the son of the Earl of Hereford, and he had been killed by Seisill ap Dyfnwal ten years earlier. Seisill was a brother of the King of Deheubarth and had a castle of his own at Llanover. Some people didn't forget what he did – and as they say, revenge is a dish best served cold.

Henry's inheritance had passed to his sister Bertha and then to her husband William de Braose, 3rd Lord of Bramber. Once William became Lord of Abergavenny, he was ready to exact revenge on behalf of his wife. So he invited Seisill, his eldest son Geoffrey and other local notables from Gwent to the castle in Abergavenny to hear a royal proclamation and have a jolly Christmas dinner. How very convivial, like gathering around to hear the monarch's Christmas message. Not only that; they were even told that they could have frank and free discussion about their grievances in an open forum. It all sounded mature and conciliatory.

Except that he proceeded to kill the lot of them.

When they arrived at Abergavenny Castle the guests surrendered their weapons – after all, it was only polite – and once inside they were murdered. De Braose and his men then rode down to Seisill's home, where they killed his 7-year-old son Cadwalladr. He thus dismantled the opposition in Gwent and earned for himself the name of 'The Ogre of Abergavenny'.

Such an abuse of the concept of 'Royal Safety' fuelled hatred and a need for revenge. A blood feud had started, which was to sour relations for generations.

1210 Corfe Castle

Mallt Walbri – Apple Cheeks

It is very strange but true that the story of William Tell, who is forced to shoot an apple from his son's head, features in Welsh folk tales.

In the Welsh version Madog is dispossessed of his land in Breconshire by the Norman William de Breos. William's wife, Matilda (or Maud) de St Valery, orders Madog to shoot an apple from the head of his youngest son. Of course he does this successfully but returns in the night with his cousin the Black Judge and they hang Maud and her son in the tower of her castle before fleeing to the Cothi Valley.

The folk story is based upon historical facts. Maud (1155–1210) was a formidable woman, known to the Welsh as Mallt Walbri. She was much admired for her beauty and her courage and trusted by her husband with managing their estates whilst he was away. She organised the defence of Painscastle and under her leadership the Normans held off an attack by Gwenwynwyn, Prince of Powys, for three weeks until reinforcements arrived. Approximately 3,000 Welshmen are said to have been killed.

William was a powerful man, a confidante of King John. But the king was to be their downfall. William seems to have gossiped loudly about John's involvement in the death of his own nephew, Arthur of Brittany. Perhaps William knew something. The king's gift to him of the Gower Peninsular may have been an attempt to buy him off. But John demanded one of their sons as a hostage to guarantee William's loyalty. Maud refused, saying loudly that she would not give her son to a man who had killed his own nephew. This was a mistake. William fled to France disguised as a beggar where he died a year later and Maud and her son fled to Ireland. They were captured and imprisoned in 1210, first in Windsor and then in Corfe Castle in Dorset. They were starved to death in a tower. It is said that when the bodies were found, it appeared that Maud had been trying to eat her dead son's cheeks before she herself died.

1237 Garth Celyn

Forgiveness

It may be strange but sadly it is true that the tomb of Siwan, now in the porch of the parish church in Beaumaris, was once used as a horse trough.

Joan (Siwan) was born in 1188, the illegitimate daughter of King John. She spent her childhood in France and was brought back in December 1203 for her marriage to Llywelyn ab Iorwerth, Prince of Gwynedd. She was 15 and her husband was 30. Their home was at Garth Celyn on the north coast of Gwynedd, on the Menai Strait.

Llywelyn (also known as Llywelyn Fawr – the Great) was a powerful figure and the marriage brought a respite in the hostilities between the English and the Welsh. But when John was succeeded by Henry III in 1218, a period of hostilities began. Llywelyn was frequently away on military campaigns.

Perhaps Siwan felt neglected? Because William de Breos, 10th Baron of Abergavenny came into her life. And as we have seen already, they were not a family for behaving themselves.

He had been taken prisoner and decided it was probably better to ally himself to Llewelyn, his captor. But there are perhaps better ways of doing this, because at Easter 1230 he was found together with Siwan in her husband's bedchamber. Llywelyn wrote to William's wife to explain what happened, saying that he had no option but to hang him. Oh and by the way, he went on, is the marriage between your daughter Isabella and my son Dafydd still on? She said yes. And so William was hanged in a place forever known as Gwern y Grog, or the Hanging Marsh.

Siwan was placed under house arrest and she gave birth to a daughter, Elen, early in 1231. The child was sent to live with other members of the family in Scotland. Once the baby had gone, Siwan was forgiven and restored as wife and princess.

She died at Garth Celyn in 1237 and Llywelyn's grief was recorded by contemporary writers. He had some sort of stroke after her death and was never the same man again. He died in 1240.

1244 The Tower of London

Gruffydd ap Llewelyn – Gaol Bird

It is appropriate that this Gruffydd ap Llewellyn, the second in the book, just like the first, has a tenuous connection with Shakespeare's *Macbeth*. Because just like Banquo, Gruffydd was not a king himself, but the begetter of kings.

This Gruffydd was the illegitimate first son of Llewelyn Fawr – Llewellyn the Great, who we have just met in the previous story.

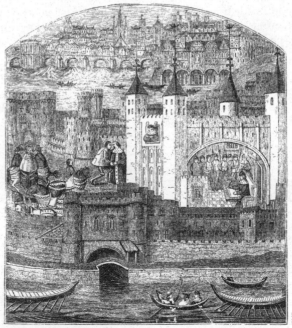

As a child he was handed over to the English as a hostage, together with the sons of other Welsh princes in the touching belief that King John would not harm them. This was a considerable misjudgement. In 1212 the other children were hanged but Gruffydd was spared and in 1215 he returned to Wales. No one has tried to explore the full extent of the psychological trauma he might have experienced and which may have shaped his future actions.

He didn't like the fact that his brother Dafydd was The Chosen One and sole heir to his father's dominions. So to keep the peace, Llewellyn Fawr imprisoned Gruffydd for six years in Deganwy Castle. It might seem a bit extreme, but parental discipline was obviously much more robust in those days.

In 1240 Gruffydd was still refusing to accept his brother Dafydd as Prince of Gwynedd. You can see a pattern forming here, I suspect. Anyway, he was imprisoned again for eleven months, this time in Criccieth Castle. When Henry III invaded, he was handed over as a hostage once again. He was imprisoned in the Tower of London for over two years. You would think that he had got used to it by now, but he made a disastrous escape attempt.

His rope made from sheets unravelled and he fell 90ft to his death from the White Tower. He didn't appear to have taken into account that his life of indolence as a hostage meant that he had put on more weight than his improvised fire escape could manage.

His greatest contribution to Welsh history occurred on those admittedly brief periods when he wasn't in prison – by establishing a brief dynasty of Welsh princes who came to such tragic ends as we will see – Llewelyn and Dafydd.

 1282 *Hawarden*

Brotherly Love

The legacy of Llewelyn Fawr faded away into horror as his descendants fought amongst themselves. A central figure in this was Dafydd ap Llewelyn, the son of Gruffydd ap Llewelyn, our gaol bird. He was never really settled, and never really sure of what he wanted. He had spent time at the court of Henry III as a hostage, and never felt part of the family, I am sure.

He and his brother Owain raised an army against their elder brother Llewelyn in 1255. They were defeated at the Battle of Bryn Derwin and were imprisoned for a while. The family seemed to have a peculiar affinity with prison. They were eventually released, and at this point Dafydd went off to join with King Henry and attacked Llewelyn again in 1267. You can see that Dafydd clearly had a number of unresolved issues in his relationship with his brother. It didn't get any better because Llewelyn was recognised by Henry III at the Treaty of Montgomery as Prince of Wales. This unresolved sibling rivalry came to haunt the Royal Family of Wales and played a terrible part in their unfolding tragedy.

I am quite sure that by this stage they had both started a serious review of their Christmas card list, because by 1274 Dafydd had allied himself with Edward I and he attacked Llewelyn once again. This brought together the fatal combination of family dysfunction and Edward I (otherwise known as Edward Longshanks), who cast such a long dark shadow over Welsh history.

The brothers were reconciled once again in 1277 following Edward's victory over the Welsh in 1277, but then Dafydd made a terrible error of judgement. He attacked the English in Hawarden Castle at Easter 1282 in Flintshire, which brought down the terrible anger of Edward I and provoked the final confrontation with the Plantagenets.

Dafydd escaped from the siege of the wonderfully dramatic Castell y Bere beneath Cader Idris in June 1283. He went on the run, but he was captured in Snowdonia and taken to Shrewsbury.

Now, a lot of his problems seem to suggest that he wasn't a boy who could make up his mind – but he didn't deserve the death allotted to him. But then, no one did.

1282 Cilmeri

Horse Play

Dafydd's ill-judged attack on Hawarden Castle in 1282 sparked a terrible conclusion. It started well, though, with a Welsh victory at the Battle of Moel y Don near Bangor on 6 November 1282. His brother Llewelyn seems to have decided to move south and arrived at Abbeycwmhir near Llandrindod Wells with a large force on 10 December.

We know for certain that Llewelyn died in the late afternoon of Friday 11 December, but the precise details are unclear. Strangely, some still believe that he spent the night in a cave near Aberedw, visiting an old lover. They admire his cunning, for his horse was shod with the shoes reversed to disguise his movements. They also believe that he was tragically killed in a chance encounter.

The truth is that Llewelyn was deceived. The key figure in his death appears to be Roger Mortimer. He laid an elaborate plot to eliminate him and in so doing paralyse the Welsh insurrection. Llewelyn left the main body of his troops when he was told that the loyalty of troops from Brecon to the English was fragile and he hoped that he could bring them on to his side. The balance of power might then swing in his direction. But the probability is that the intelligence wasn't genuine; It was the final piece in an elaborate plan. He was ambushed at Cilmeri near the River Irfon at dusk on Friday, 11 December 1282 and all of his party were killed in a brief engagement. In such a moment, history changed forever.

When the prince's head was removed, so was the head of the Welsh forces. Fortified by their success in this ambush, the English-led forces attacked the leaderless Welsh early the next morning and slaughtered them.

1283 Shrewsbury

The Welsh Die Nasty – Dafydd ap Gruffydd

King Edward I's outrage at Dafydd's behaviour was such that he designed a punishment for him harsher than any previous form of capital punishment. Llewelyn had already been tricked, trapped and eliminated and Dafydd was described by the king as 'the last of a treacherous lineage'.

It is strange to think that the idea of high treason was invented for him. Before Dafydd it wasn't a crime to oppose the king. But the last Welsh Prince of Wales managed to change all that.

On 3 October 1283 he was executed. He was dragged through the streets of Shrewsbury, hanged, disembowelled and hacked into quarters. His head was displayed on London Bridge next to that of his brother. Geoffrey of Shrewsbury was paid 20s for carrying this out. Whether his health and safety qualifications were sufficient to allow him to perform such an awful task is not recorded.

Edward effectively eliminated an entire dynasty – emasculating Welsh political power and influence for centuries to come. Branches of the family kept the fires of rebellion alive – Madog ap Llewelyn led a revolt in 1295 and so did Dafydd Goch, perhaps an illegitimate son of Dafydd, but these were the dying embers. Dafydd ap Gruffyd's unmarried daughters were sent off to be nuns, and the fate of his two sons provides an awful postscript to this story.

Owain and Llewellyn were taken to Bristol Castle. Llewellyn died in 1287 but Owain lived on, poor boy. He was last reported alive in 1325, when he would have been 50. He had been a captive for thirty-eight years. Edward had instructed that 'a strong house within the castle to be repaired as soon as possible and to make a wooden cage bound with iron in that house in which Owain might be enclosed'. (*The accounts of Bristol Castle*)

It is so, so chilling.

No charm hath life our youth beside
And youth can but an hour abide

– Welsh proverb

 1284 *Pwllheli*

Herring Aid

Pwllheli 1284 – and not a caravan in sight. And how do we know this strange but undeniably true fact? Because the victorious Edward I requested an inventory of his inheritance after defeating Prince Llewelyn and effectively taking possession of Wales.

It was all meticulously written down. Llewelyn had had a residence there, maintained by the men of Pwllheli, who each gave three or four days' labour a year. He also owned a mill where the locals were obliged to grind their corn in return for an annual payment of flour. They also had to pay in return for a house and a plot of land, though this was normally in the form of wheat or herring.

The inventory outlined each individual's wealth. The wealthiest resident was Iorwerth, who had three oxen, nine cows, two horses and some sacks of flour and wheat – worth a total of £4 7s. In fact, throughout the whole of Gwynedd, there were very few people who had property worth more than £5.

Madog ab Einon had seven nets, Thomas ap Robin a fishing boat and two nets, while Goronwy Gwta had a boat and three nets. Another resident only had a horse. Pwllheli kept itself alive by working together and sharing their resources; they had little use for money. They lived in huts made out of mud and wattle, along what is now the High Street. The highest point was the prince's place, on top of a mound.

Slowly this life would change. Money as a medium of exchange would be used more extensively to facilitate trade at markets and at fairs. This would lead inevitably to the end of the rural economy and the beginnings of a taxation system, something which the Welsh have always been reluctant to embrace.

 1340 *Monmouthshire*

The Longbow

The great successes of the English in the Hundred Years War against France were largely due to the Welsh archers who came in the main from South Wales, especially Monmouthshire.

It took enormous strength to draw a longbow and required years of training. They would begin as boys, with the bows gradually becoming bigger. They were taught to use their bodies to push against the bow, not just to draw the string. It led to physical changes in the archers themselves, who developed enlarged left arms. This was hardly surprising given the draw weight required, which was normally in excess of 80lbs. Practise was compulsory and no range was allowed to be less than 220 yards by order of the king.

Welsh bows were made of elm and often appeared unfinished. But they were made from a single piece of wood for strength, not looks. The strings were made from hemp, flax or silk.

When fighting the English back home, they ambushed their enemy and then fired at point blank range, straight through most types of armour. But when fighting for the English against the French, their effective range was at least 200 yards. It was hard to hit an individual but easy to hit an army. Each archer had about seventy arrows, which they stuck in the ground by their side, thus increasing the possibility of wound infection. Boys ran around replenishing supplies. Archers would fire huge volleys at the rate of about six a minute, though they couldn't keep this up for too long. They were usually deployed behind stakes and ditches to disrupt any charges, but they were vulnerable if they were attacked before these had been prepared.

It was the horses that were the most vulnerable in an arrow storm. Wounded horses could spread enormous amounts of chaos – and an unseated knight was often easy meat for Welsh archers with a hammer and a dagger.

Eventually French tactics finally changed. They started to attack before the archers were properly deployed behind protective stakes and ditches. Soon the longbow was replaced by the gun, which could be used with less training and made a more impressive noise. But not as good. It might seem strange, but it is true that English commanders believed the longbow would have been more effective, more reliable and more accurate than the muskets used at the Battle of Waterloo in 1815.

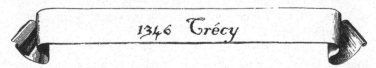

1346 Crécy

Cross Bowmen

It was the Welsh archers who did it – as they liked to do. Destroying a French army. It was what they were good at. On this occasion the English army under Edward III became trapped as they marched through France. The French tracked their movements across Normandy and finally forced a confrontation at the village of Crécy-en-Ponthieu in the Pas de Calais.

There were about 10,000 soldiers in the English army, of whom about half were archers. The majority of those were Welsh. They had already marched 300 miles and waded across the Somme at low tide, pursued by a huge French army. The French finally turned up at midday on 26 August 1346 and started their attack almost immediately, without taking the time to organise themselves. The English had been waiting for them and dug ditches to disrupt a French assault.

Crossbowmen from Genoa were sent to start the battle, but rain made their bowstrings wet and caused them to stretch, so their first volley fell short. The Welsh had stuffed their own bowstrings in their shirts or their caps, and so kept them dry. And whilst the crossbow was powerful and effective, it took a long time to load. Usually the crossbowmen had screens behind which they sheltered to prime their weapons. These had been left behind in the baggage train, so they were extremely vulnerable. Withering fire from the Welsh set them running backwards, straight into the first line of French knights going forwards. They in their turn started to attack the Genoese as pasta-eating surrender monkeys. It was suddenly chaotic. The first French line impeded the second French line – and all the time under a hail of arrows. The French historian Jean de Venette wrote that the arrows were 'coming from heaven and the skyes which were formerly bright, suddenly darkened' (*The Chronicle of Jean de Venette*).

French knights, immobile in their heavy armour after being brought to earth by horses wounded in the arrow storm, were easy meat for Welshmen. They did their terrible business with hammers and the sort of knives that slipped easily through joints in the armour. It was a complete disaster. Around 4,000 French knights died. English casualties are estimated at about 300. And later at Agincourt, the Welsh would continue to corner the market in improbable victories.

During the Battle of Crécy, one of the casualties was blind King John of Bohemia, who went into battle strapped to his horse. The Black Prince, knighted by his father Edward III just before the fighting began, adopted King John's emblem – three white feathers and the motto *Ich dien* (I serve) – which is still the emblem of the Prince of Wales.

+ Cnapan is an early variant of a team ball game, generally
  confined to West Wales. There were few rules and games
  seemed to have involved the entire male population of
  two rival villages. Most contestants played on foot, though
  the well-off would play on horseback. It was regarded as
  decent practise for warfare. The wooden ball was soaked
  or boiled in oil for a long time in order to make it slippery,
  thereby introducing a frisson of uncertainty to throwing
  and catching. It was certainly played in medieval times and
  probably began centuries earlier than that. The object was
  to take the ball to the church in your own village, by any
  possible means. Games could last all day, though they usually
  ended when the players lost interest and had hit as many
  people as pride required. There was no referee, merely the
  occasional shout of 'Heddwch!' (Peace!) to halt play and stop
  anyone getting seriously hurt. It is no longer played, since
  insurance premiums for players are a little heavy. However, it
  is suggested that it was once revived in the North of England
  when an international match was played between Wales and
  England. The Welsh won easily, since they omitted to tell the
  English what to do.

  'Playing at football is and was a very popular custom
  amongst the Cambrians, in which game they exerted
  themselves, at times, even to the loss of a limb …
  this football playing frequently led to petty wars, and
  seldom terminated without bloodshed …' (W. Howells,
  Cambrian Superstitions, 1831)

+ Apparently in Bosherston (Pembrokeshire), the local cure for
  whooping cough involved taking the afflicted to a limestone
  cave at Bullslaughter Bay and holding them over a bubbling
  cauldron of boiled seaweed until they were sick.

+ The Town Hall in Cardiff was built on the High Street in 1331.
  It was also used as the first Market Hall.

+ The poet Deio ap Ieuan Du died in 1480. He composed
  the motto that appears on the Cardiff coat of arms, which
  translates as 'The Red Dragon will show the way'.

When the English besieged Caen in 1346, some French defenders exposed their backsides from the battlements as an act of contempt since Englishmen were rumoured to have tails. The aim of the Welsh archers was unerring and the Frenchmen took no further part in the hostilities.

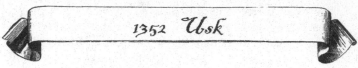

1352 Usk

Adam of Usk and the Sexing Chair

Adam made a place for himself as a historian and then found a place in this book through his assiduous research into the ancient sport of pope sexing.

Adam, born in Usk in 1352, studied at Oxford where he became a Doctor of Law. He worked as a university lecturer and then in the archbishop's court in Canterbury. He went to Rome where he worked for a couple of popes as papal chaplain and where he was able to pursue some unusual lines of historical research before he returned to Wales. He is remembered for his *Chronicles*, a history of 1377–1421. But we remember him here because of the work he did on Pope Joan.

Now the Catholic Church still denies that there was ever a female pope, but Adam was happy to repeat the rumour. The story was that a talented and devoted woman disguised herself as a man and was elected pope. Sadly, whilst in procession through Rome she went into labour and her gender thus revealed, she was killed by an angry mob, tied to her horse and dragged through the streets.

This is supposed to have happened in AD 850 and she was left off the list of popes out of shame. The absence of any real evidence that she ever actually existed is the only proof anyone ever needs in any sort of conspiracy theory. What greater proof could there ever be than no evidence at all? In fact Adam stated that she was an Englishwoman called Agnes, but it was so long ago that anything was possible.

He writes that in order to stop it happening again, all subsequent popes were examined carefully. They were asked to sit upon a stool called the *sella stercoraria* which had a strategically placed hole. Through this a cardinal could handle the goods (or not) and establish the gender of the pope, uttering the traditional phrase *Duos habet et bene pendentes*, which your local Latin scholar can translate for you.

Adam died in Usk in 1430.

1376 Hereford

Border Trouble

By the end of the fourteenth century, the Welsh Borders were not a good place to be. There was significant unrest everywhere, fuelled by the trauma of the Black Death, but there was a particular increase in lawlessness along the borders.

Complaints were made in Parliament in 1376, and the following year prominent landowners in Herefordshire petitioned the king to complain. They reported that bands of Welshmen would appear in groups of up to a hundred. 'They have beaten people and maimed several: more they have killed in the houses…and taken their chattels, committing such brutalities and threats in the county as far as the city of Hereford'. (Thomas Wright Longmans, *A History of Ludlow and Its Neighbourhood*, 1852)

Another complaint was about the harassment and detention of English merchants who crossed the border to trade. In 1378 Bristol, Hereford, Gloucester, Worcester and Shrewsbury all complained to Parliament about the disruption and distress their people experienced. The Welsh weren't too keen on Englishmen who went into Wales to recover unpaid debts either, but then they have never been keen to accommodate debt collectors.

The situation was reflected in a law which prohibited Welshmen from buying or holding land along the border. Those who had owned land were believed to have supported the bands of raiders who crossed the border: 'In war-like array, [they] perpetrate their daily diverse man-slaughters, felonies and other transgressions and enormities, and then retreat in haste to the other side of the border, beyond the jurisdiction of the magistrates of the counties in which the offence was committed.' (Longmans, *A History of Ludlow*)

Retaliatory measures were authorised. In 1394 it was declared lawful that if any of a town's citizens was taken off into Wales, the town citizens were entitled to arrest a Welshman until their own man was released. Revenge attacks took place too. There were raids when former soldiers crossed the Dee, where they took livestock, trampled crops and assaulted and robbed peasants.

This breakdown in law and order created the context in which the Glyndŵr revolt would suddenly burst into life in 1400.

✦ The forests were an important part of the economy.
They supplied food and hunting and were jealously guarded.
Foresters had a reputation for ruthlessness. They could levy tolls, fine trespassers and punish poachers. They could impose fines and amputate arms if these fines were not paid.

 1382 *Llandovery*

Good Sense

These days at Llandovery station you can get a train which takes you either to Shrewsbury or Llanelli – which is as good a reason for staying put as you could want.

Of course, there have always been superior attractions in Llandovery; not least the Physicians of Myddfai, who had considerable mystical powers and could probably have cured you of most things, even the desire to take the train to Llanelli.

Myddfai is a small village and community with its very own myths and legends and there has always been a sense that in some way the people of Myddfai retained contact with the essential truths of the past that the modern world had misplaced.

The physicians were a dynasty of talented doctors, homeopaths and herbalists. Their knowledge was passed down through 1,000 years. They were a repository of ancient remedies, generally made from natural produce grown in the area. And so they could fix your headache, your sunburn, the pain in your leg, coughs and sneezes.

Some claim that Myddfai was the birthplace of modern medicine, which does appear a little over-inflated. But certainly the village became a centre for medical help and people came from all over the country to be cured. It was a place of learning and of pilgrimage.

Its origins lie in myth; the story tells of a local farmer, who married the Lady of the Lake. He beat her once too often, so she left him and submerged herself and their cattle. She returned to her sons and instructed them in the life-giving properties of natural remedies, their power augmented quite naturally by their fairy blood, inherited from an other-worldly mother.

This is all laid out in the famous *Red Book of Hergest*, an ancient manuscript from 1382, full of poetry and those herbal remedies handed down from the estranged mother to her son Rhiwallon Feddyg. It was medical practice based upon observation and upon the not unreasonable assumption that the patient was responsible for their own health; so it emphasised moderation and good sense. Simple solutions, the sort that are timeless – moderation in all things and plenty of sleep. It is what the reputation of the Physicians of

Myddfai has always been based upon. Strangely the last man to claim direct descent from Rhiwallon was Dr Rice Williams from Aberystwyth, who died aged 85 in 1842.

In the fourteenth century the Black Death came to call on Builth Wells. It is said that the people living in the local countryside left food and provisions for the townspeople on the banks of a stream to the west of the town. While the plague was a terrifying and deadly threat, the money generated by trade with the town was not something that could be ignored. In return, Builth Wells' inhabitants threw money into the water to prevent the spread of the plague. As a result the stream became known as 'Nant Yr Arian' or 'the Money Brook'. It is interesting that exactly the same story is told about the village of Eyam in Derbyshire, which isolated itself when the plague struck there 200 years later. The only difference is that there they paid for their provisions with coins which had been soaked in vinegar.

1400 Paris

Have Bow, Will Travel

Wales had always been a valuable recruiting area for soldiers to serve in the English army. They served throughout the Hundred Years' War and established quite a reputation.

Lodewyk van Velthem from Ghent described them in his chronicles. They went around bare-legged, wearing linen tunics. They used bows, arrows and swords rather like a rapier, which were called *twca*. They also carried javelins and billhooks.

Unsurprisingly, they had a well-developed reputation for lawlessness. They were feared because they would take whatever they needed from the local population, without much regard for which side they were fighting on. They were also renowned for their drunkenness and debauchery. Regrettably perhaps, a prostitute in medieval Paris was sometimes called a *galloise* after their most loyal customers. It is true – though in the circumstances, not especially strange.

Back in Wales, the community had a long tradition of respect for military action which reflected deeply ingrained tribal roots, but constant fighting created a sense of brutality and an acceptance of violence. Admirable qualities in some circumstances, but not at home when there are jobs to be done.

Recruitment into the army would withdraw from society a body of aggressive and reckless young men, but problems would emerge once they returned home and had to be reintegrated into society in some way. Rural life was not always exciting enough and ex-soldiers would often become rootless and criminal, taking to the hills and the forests. At the same time, if you were an outlaw you could earn a pardon through military service. As you can see there was the potential for the endless recycling of criminality and anti-social attitudes.

After Glyndŵr's defeat, Welsh soldiers, especially longbowmen, enlisted in the English armies on the Continent. In Henry V's Agincourt campaign, over 500 men from South Wales served under John Merbury and acquired a reputation for terrible ferocity. As mercenaries though, it is no surprise that there was a small number of Welshmen fighting on the French side too.

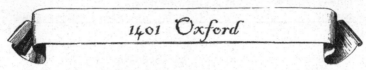

1401 Oxford

Students are Revolting

The Glyndŵr rebellion provoked a large number of punitive laws against the Welsh between 1401 and 1402. If you consider that considerable racial enmity still existed following centuries of conflict, it could be no surprise that such laws would make things even worse.

+ No Englishman could be convicted of any crime if he was accused by a Welshman
+ No Englishman could be tried by a Welsh jury
+ Any Welshman who raided the English counties was to be regarded as outside the law – an outlaw in effect, and without the protection of the law
+ No Englishman or woman should marry or consort with the Welsh.
+ No English child should be fostered amongst the Welsh
+ Englishmen married to Welshwomen were to be put out of office
+ No Welshman bearing arms could enter a town or castle or even use the highways
+ Welshmen were forbidden to hold castles or fortified houses
+ They were barred from holding official posts like a justice or constable
+ No food could be carried into Wales without a licence
+ The Welsh were forbidden from gathering together

All this legislation merely served to make the atmosphere more hostile. There seemed to be an assault on Welsh culture too, with rumours circulating that the Welsh language was to be banned. Welsh bards were also accused of being subversive 'because their divinations, lies and exhortations are partly cause of the insurrection and rebellion in Wales'. (Adam of Usk, *Chronicon Adae de Usk*)

Welshmen in England – like labourers and deserting soldiers – returned home to join the rebellion. So did Welsh students at Oxford and Cambridge. In 1402, the Sheriff of Oxford was asked to investigate allegations of seditious meetings by Welsh students. It wasn't the last time it would happen either.

This legislation remained in force for a long time and all statutes against Welshmen were once again confirmed in 1447. In fact it was only with the invention of rugby that the Welsh persuaded themselves that they could get their own back.

✦ In the early part of the fifteenth century, the Welsh regarded themselves as a defeated and oppressed people. A hatred of the English is a recurrent theme of the poetry of this time.

✦ The Glyndŵr rebellion not only devastated the Welsh economy, leaving areas depopulated and ruined; it also destroyed the culture. During the reign of Elizabeth I, regret was expressed at the destruction of books and libraries that had occurred.

✦ During the Glyndŵr rebellion, seven Welsh rebels were imprisoned in the Tower of London and fifty-seven in Newgate Gaol.

 1402 *Pilleth*

Picking Sides

Pilleth near Knighton is the site of the battle which marked Owain Glyndŵr's most famous victory on 22 June 1402.

Edmund Mortimer, aged 26, took an army of at least 2,000 men to confront the Welsh who were at the top of Bryn Glas, a hill with a 1 in 4 gradient. The Welsh may have looked an insubstantial force, but

Mortimer could see only some of the troops. Half of the Welsh force had been hidden in a wood to the left.

The two sides began by exchanging archery fire. But the Welsh had the high ground and therefore greater range. The English took heavy casualties before they could even start up the steep slope. When they did charge, they were disorganised and ragged and easily picked off. On one flank Mortimer had deployed some conscripted Welsh archers of his own. However, pretty soon they could see the way the battle was developing.

So, perhaps sensibly, they decided to switch sides. It was a decisive moment.

The Welsh charged down the slope to crash into the struggling English and the hidden troops emerged from the trees. Soon, those who could retired from the field in disorder. St Mary's church, the dividing line between the two forces, was burning. Casualties were huge: 800 English dead – perhaps more – and Edmund Mortimer captured. Stories are told about the horrible mutilation of the English dead, carried out by the women in the Welsh camp, a story Shakespeare was happy to repeat in *Henry IV Part I*.

Mortimer was held for ransom but Henry IV refused to pay. He was, allegedly, strapped for cash. The potential difficulties this might have caused Mortimer were easily solved. Following the example of the Welsh archers, he too switched sides. He signed a pact with Glyndŵr to overthrow Henry. This was a high point of the rebellion. When the English came back the Welsh were trapped in the castles, their resources quickly exhausted. Owain Glyndŵr's own lands in the north of Wales were ransacked and the area he controlled shrank rapidly.

The site of the Battle of Pilleth in 1402 is marked by four Wellingtonia trees. They were planted by the MP for Radnor, Sir Richard Green-Price, when drainage work on the hill started to uncover bodies in the nineteenth century.

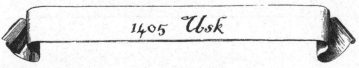

1405 Usk

Yellow Pond

Dafydd ap Llewelyn ap Hywel was better known as Dafydd Gam – or Crooked David. This was a reference to his limp and perhaps also to his loss of an eye. It could also be a reference to his behaviour, which seemed calculated to upset everyone. His countrymen said that he was 'small in stature and deformed in person'. (George Borrow, *Wild Wales: Its People, Language and Scenery*, 1862)

He was probably born near Brecon, perhaps in 1351, and claimed descent from the earliest Welsh kings. However, he remained fiercely loyal to the English throne and led opposition in Wales. It is believed that he was leader of the troops who defeated Glyndŵr's men at the Battle of Pwll Melyn near Usk in 1405. This proved to be a key moment in the rebellion. Over 300 Welshmen including important leaders were executed in front of the castle after the battle. It took place to the north of the town, at Castle Oak pond, and it is said that the yellow colour (*melyn*) came from the number of bodies dumped in it. Certainly many skeletons were found when it was drained.

Dafydd was rewarded with a gift of land in Cardigan, which had been confiscated from the rebels. In 1412 he was captured by Glyndŵr's men and was ransomed by the king himself. He had to swear an oath not to oppose Glyndŵr in the future. On his release he told the king where Glyndŵr was and attacked the Welsh. In response, Dafydd's estates were burned. Previously in 1404 he had tried to assassinate Glyndŵr at Machynthleth, but had been generously released. You imagine that Glyndŵr was having second thoughts about such generosity. He became 'chief enemy and traitor' – a title of which you suspect he was proud.

He died at Agincourt in 1415. He was sent out to observe the French and reported famously that there were 'enough to kill, enough to capture and enough to run away'. It is said that he saved King Henry V's life during the fighting but was himself fatally wounded. Henry knighted him moments before he died in the cold French mud.

> ✦ 'There are three incitements to revenge; the wailing of female relatives, and seeing the bier of their relatives and seeing the grave of their relative without compensation.'
> (Sara Elin Roberts, *The Legal Triads of Medieval Wales*, 2011)

Guto'r Glyn

Guto became one of the greatest poets in medieval Wales. He was born Gruffudd ap Siancyn and came from humble origins; a boy from the hills who succeeded through his talent alone. He was big and strong, bearded and bald. Rivals described him as unattractive and with a nose like a billhook.

Guto became very well known because of his mastery of *cywydd mab*, poetry written in praise of his rich patrons. He had a number of high-profile sponsors. One of his patrons was Abbot Rhys of Strata Florida, who died in prison in Carmarthen after failing to collect enough taxes for the English king. Guto describes him 'as the eagle of the feast', presumably suggesting that he took no prisoners at the medieval buffet.

He was a soldier who fought in France during the Hundred Years War, and later worked as a drover for a while. During this time, he was engaged in driving a flock of sheep for the parson of Corwen to England for sale. Unfortunately, he managed to lose them somewhere, and became quite stroppy in a spat with another poet about it. He was disappointed that a rival poet, Tudur Penllyn, wouldn't help him. In return Tudur accused him of stealing the sheep to give them to his wife in Oswestry. Poets clearly lived life on the edge in those days.

Guto fought on the side of the House of York in the Wars of the Roses, but wrote in praise of Rhys ap Thomas, who – as the Welsh have always known – killed Richard III. Guto's poem, often overlooked by English historians, explains precisely what happened to Richard at Bosworth. Whilst there was a belief that Richard's fate would always remain unclear, Guto writes that Rhys 'killed the boar; shaved his head'. (The original Welsh line reads 'Lladd y baedd, eilliodd ei ben'.) The discovery of Richard's body indicated quite clearly that he had been scalped. Historians should just listen to the poets.

> ✦ 'Three things that every man is entitled to take without the permission of another; water that is not in a vessel, a stone that is not in use, and a fire from a hollow tree.' (Sara Elin Roberts, *The Legal Triads of Medieval Wales*, 2011)

The Mud of France

Once again the Welsh archers came to the rescue in battle, though the French made their own special contribution to their defeat at Agincourt.

The French were still strangely convinced by the full frontal assault. It was a simple and unsophisticated tactic. The shockwave of the heavily armoured cavalry charge and then hand-to-hand combat. It hadn't worked at either Crécy or Poitiers and it didn't work here.

The English army, led by Henry V, had been in France for three months. They had besieged and taken the port of Harfleur and then marched north across Normandy towards Calais to go home. It was a difficult march – 260 miles in twenty days. They were tracked all the way by the French and their progress was hindered by dysentery which ran unchecked (if you see what I mean) through the army. It was an exhausted and weakened army that was finally forced to stand and fight at Agincourt on 25 October 1415.

The French army was much bigger and well rested, and the English were fatalistic. The French celebrated an anticipated victory and squabbled about who would be in the front line with the greatest chance of capturing English knights as hostages and generate a cash profit.

The bedraggled English knelt in the rain and took pieces of mud into their mouths to prepare for death. Henry tried to rally his troops and addressed them without spurs to show that he would fight on foot amongst them.

However, they had a better position on the narrow and muddy battlefield – and this proved to be the key issue. The French were compressed by forests on either side and the battlefield was quickly churned and became impassable. The second French line became trapped behind the first. The archers killed the horses and the heavily armoured French were unable to move in the mud. Some drowned. The Welsh archers could move amongst them easily with their daggers and help themselves to what they could carry.

It was a remarkably short encounter; a couple of hours at the most. Estimates suggest that the English suffered 450 casualties whilst the French lost 4,000, including three dukes, eight counts and an archbishop.

> ✦ On their way through Northern France towards Agincourt, the Welsh archers suffered a virulent attack of dysentery and marched naked below the waist. There were probably advantages to marching at the front.

1470 Llangynidr

Fat David the Otter

A particular region which acquired a reputation for lawlessness was Brecon. Their neighbours were convinced that they regarded cattle stealing as an acceptable occupation, perhaps with its own range of qualifications and career structure for all I know. But it certainly made them very unpopular. They were always nipping over the borders to help themselves to whatever they could find.

In 1470 some men of Brecon went on a raid as far as Ogmore in Glamorgan. They turned up at the end of September and killed a man called Jenkin Mathew in Cowbridge. They then smashed up the Michaelmas Fair in Ewenny. This combination of events caused justifiable upset and the locals chased the raiding party until they caught them at Llangynidr near Crickhowell. The skirmish (or perhaps battle) was a vicious affair and many of the Brecon men were killed, including their leader Dafydd Tew Dwrgi – a name which translates wonderfully as Fat David the Otter.

The survivors ran away to the north and Dafydd ap Jenkin from nearby Braich y Cymer loaded up his cart with the Brecon dead and took them to Llangynidr churchyard, where they were buried in a mass grave – or as the locals described it, a great heap. The mound over them could be seen for many years at the north end of the churchyard.

There were two consequences of this particular unpleasantness. One was that the Brecon poet Hywel Dafi wrote a poem in an attempt to bring about reconciliation. After all, their very own saints, Cynog from Brecon and Cadog from Glamorgan, had been big chums. The two regions had previously shown a healthy interest in plunder. Why let a little disagreement drive a wedge between them?

The second consequence was that the Michaelmas Fair was moved from Ewenny to St Bride's Down.

+ English and Welsh law differed significantly in respect of capital punishment. The Welsh believed that monetary compensation was more appropriate than execution. Where homicide was concerned, such blood money was called *galanas*. When the harpist Sion Eos killed a man in a pub brawl in around 1450 he was found guilty and hanged. His friend the poet Dafydd ap Edmwnds wrote a notable piece called 'Marwnad Sion Eos', in which he attacked the jury for using the laws of London rather than the laws of Wales.

 1485 Bosworth

Rhys ap Thomas

Whatever you think of Rhys ap Thomas, the phrase 'I told you so' springs to mind. It is quite simple. Everyone around him knew he had killed Richard III on the battlefield at Bosworth. He was famous for it. Henry Tudor regarded him as a national hero as a result. This claim to fame was vindicated when they dug up the king's body in a

car park in Leicester in 2012. It was clear then what had happened –
and what had happened was exactly what the Welsh had been saying
ever since 1485.

Rhys was probably born in Llandeilo in 1449. It was a time of
turmoil and civil war. Rhys' family supported the Lancastrian side
and vainly defended Carreg Cennen Castle in a siege. Defeat saw
him driven into exile in Burgundy. There are worse fates …

On his return Rhys appeared to side with Richard, who had
usurped the throne, but secretly maintained contact with Henry
Tudor. When Henry landed near Dale, Rhys joined him. The Bishop
of St David absolved him of his obligation to Richard by persuading
him that he should lie down and allow Henry to step over him. This
rather humiliating procedure was managed when Rhys stood under
Mullock Bridge while Henry marched over it. Allegedly.

Rhys played a vital role in the defeat of Richard at Bosworth on 22 August 1485 – a turning point in British history. Richard was unhorsed and surrounded, after the Welsh troops resisted the initial attack. He was killed with an axe or a halberd when the back of his head was sliced off. Did Rhys do it? If he didn't, Henry still knew that he owed him a huge debt of gratitude. Rhys was certainly knighted on the battlefield and made Governor of Wales.

He was granted land across South Wales and died at Carmarthen Priory in 1525. The images on his tomb, now in St Peter's church, show the death of Richard quite clearly.

+ The Battle of Bosworth was regarded as a Welsh victory; indeed it was believed that the accession of Henry Tudor represented the triumph of the ancient prophesies of Merlin.

+ Every English monarch since Henry VII has descended from a Welshman.

 1497 Labrador

Amerike – Newnamedland

If you want to feel the warm glow of Welsh nationalistic pride then consider that there are those amongst you who believe that America is named after one of your own. Those – like me – less fortunate than you (i.e. not Welsh) have always believed that the continent was named after a Florentine sailor called Amerigo Vespucci. But it was, so it goes, named after a senior customs official from Bristol.

His name was Richard Amerike, an important money-man who was the chief sponsor of the voyages of Giovanni Cabotto (also known as John Cabot), the famous navigator who set out from Bristol in 1497 and became the first recorded European to set foot on American soil, three years before Vespucci.

Cabot set off with letters from Henry VII, saying that he could claim lands on the king's behalf. He reached Labrador and mapped the coastline, before returning to plan his second and more extensive expedition. It took him thirty-four days to get there and two weeks to get back, bringing with him the jawbone of a whale.

Amerike's name derives from the Welsh ap Meuric. He was born in 1445 at Weston under Penyard, near Ross-on-Wye, descended from the Earls of Gwent. He became Sheriff of Bristol and the King's Customs Officer. As a major sponsor of Cabot, he provided the wood to build Cabot's ship the *Matthew* from his family estate at Ross. And as I am sure you have guessed, his family's coat of arms featured stars and stripes. And if you are a true believer, then this cannot be a coincidence.

There is strong evidence that fishermen from Bristol had already started to visit the fishing grounds off Newfoundland so it is not a surprise that they should want to support further explorations of a lucrative resource. Neither is it a surprise that Cabot might wish to recognise the contribution of one of his sponsors by sticking his name on a map.

I sense that you might be struggling here – but stop for a moment and consider this. It is only royalty who have countries named after them on the basis of their first names. And Amerigo was no royal. The rest of us have to make do with our surname if we want to appear in an atlas.

Just like Amerike…

1507 *Bacton*

Blanche Parry – Nursey

Blanche (1507–1590) was an extraordinary and very influential woman who survived the intricacies and uncertainties of life at the Tudor court through her unswerving loyalty to Queen Elizabeth. Her name was Blanche ferch Harry or Blanche ap Harry and she came from a prominent border family in Bacton, Herefordshire, with a Welsh father and an English mother. She was brought up in a Welsh cultural environment in Newcourt, and the family was referred to in a poem by the Welsh bard Guto'r Glyn. Naturally she was bilingual.

The family was very well connected. Consequently she was taken to court with her aunt, Lady Troy, who was Lady Mistress to Henry VIII's children, Edward VI and Elizabeth. Blanche was 25 and one of her first tasks was rocking Elizabeth's cradle. From that moment they were rarely separated. She allegedly taught Elizabeth some Welsh and she attended her in prison following the execution of her mother, Anne Boleyn. She was with her through her troubles, her dangers and her triumphs. She was at the centre of court life.

In 1558, on Elizabeth's succession, she was appointed Chief Gentlewoman of the Privy Chamber and effectively controlled access to the queen. She was also in charge of her jewels, her papers and her clothes. She supervised the queen's linen and also apparently looked after the queen's ferret. Tough job.

Blanche acquired land in Herefordshire, Wales and Yorkshire but was never really interested in her own advancement. She was dependable and discreet, a trusted confidante – and that was enough for her. She was respected by everyone at court – a singular achievement in such complicated times.

Although she prepared a tomb for herself in Bacton church, it remained unused. Blanche became blind in her old age and died, unmarried, in February 1590 in her 80s. On her death she was buried in St Margaret's in Westminster at the queen's expense. As her unused epitaph in Bacton says, 'With maiden Queen a maid did end my life.'

1512 Tenby

It All Adds Up

Robert Recorde is one of those Welshmen who has touched the lives of everyone, even if they don't know it.

He was born in Tenby and went to Oxford University to study medicine. His first publication was *The Urinal of Physick* (1547), an essential text that explored how you could diagnose illness from the condition of the patient's urine. Recorde, however, was most interested in mathematics and in navigation; like everyone he was keen to find a north–west passage.

In 1549 he became Controller of the Royal Mint in Bristol. This was not a job without its dangers. The previous incumbent had been sent to the Tower, and Recorde himself was imprisoned for sixty days for giving money to the wrong people. He was also Controller of Mines and Money in Ireland. He clashed with the Earl of Pembroke in a dispute about mining and smelting rights at Pentyrch, near Cardiff. Pembroke sued Recorde for libel in October 1556 and was awarded £1,000 in damages which Recorde couldn't pay. He was imprisoned and died in 1558. Ironically in 1570 his estate was awarded £1,000 for his work in Ireland.

He wrote a number of books – *The Pathway to Knowledge* (about geometry), *The Gate of Knowledge*, *The Castle of Knowledge* (about astronomy), and *The Treasure of Knowledge*. He clearly had no time for modest titles. These books were written in English, and were intended to be simple and accessible. He invented English mathematical terms which sadly did not catch on – like 'cinkangle' for pentagon, and 'siseangle' for hexagon. But his greatest contribution was the equals sign: =. He got fed-up with writing 'is equal to' and designed the new symbol because, as he said, he could think of nothing more equal than two parallel lines of the same length.

So simple and so universal. Tenby's pride.

+ Robert Recorde invented the word to describe a number to the eighth power – 'zenzizenzizenic' – for which he needs to be remembered, even if he is forgotten for everything else. In his book *The Whetstone of Witte* he manages to explain that it 'doth represent the square of squares squaredly.' I couldn't put it better myself.

 1519 Caernarvon

A Beef Dinner

In the early part of the sixteenth century the government of North Wales was in the hands of Sir William Griffiths of Penrhyn, who acted as chamberlain.

It wasn't a successful appointment.

Whilst his personal bard Lewys Mon composed poems saying how wonderful he was, suppressing bandits across North Wales and generally being the shining light of civilisation, others were less impressed. In January 1519 the Council of the Marches heard compelling accusations from eighteen prominent residents of Caernarvonshire and Anglesey.

They accused Sir William of supporting outlaws and releasing murderers from prison. They also stated that he had a private army of at least 500 men and that he constantly abused his position of authority for his own gain through intimidation and extortion.

They went on to say that he had confiscated the property of people in Merionethshire after accusing them of sheltering outlaws. Sir William was also accused of levying a *cymhortha* on Anglesey and Caernarvonshire. This represented a compulsory contribution of almost 1,000 cows to assist with the celebrations of his daughter's wedding. Clearly there were a lot of guests.

He denied it, of course. Sir William replied to the accusations by saying that they had been made as the result of the 'enticement of diverse malicious persons'. He was particularly agitated by the evidence of one of his accusers, Gruffydd ap Morris. Sir William said that his accusations had been motivated simply by revenge. He had turned down Gruffydd's application for ownership of a farm on the grounds that this was where his brother sheltered with his band of bandits.

By June the Council arrived at a judgement. Sir William Griffiths was told not to levy any more *cymhortha* and was told that he couldn't hold any other public office without the express consent of the king. His actions were to be more carefully monitored but he remained in office.

Gruffydd ap Morris, meanwhile, was committed to the Fleet Prison in London.

+ In 1521 Griffith ap Evan ap Dafydd – a cruel and notable
  outlaw – was caught and taken to Shrewsbury where he was
  tried, condemned and hanged, drawn and quartered. His cattle
  had been stolen and as a result he had looked for revenge
  on the family of those who he said had stolen his animals.
  The town chronicles tell us that a labourer was paid 5*d* for
  sticking his head on a post over the town gate towards Wales
  to the terror and example of other like felons and rebels.

 1527 *Knighton*

Here Comes the Mirror Man

John Dee (1527–1608), the legendary mathematician and astrologer,
was probably born near Knighton in Radnorshire. He claimed to be
a descendant of Rhodri Mawr, Prince of Wales. Perhaps he was, but
he was also the model for the character of Prospero in Shakespeare's
The Tempest. He was always regarded with suspicion because of the
things he knew. In 1583 a mob tried to destroy his library, believing
he was a black magician.

He was a Cambridge graduate, a fellow of Trinity College.
He became a special advisor to Queen Elizabeth. He believed that
numbers were the basis of all things and the key to all knowledge.

Astrology and alchemy were regarded as perfectly acceptable
pursuits at the time, but his belief in his ability to contact the spirit
world was not. Much appears to have been based upon optical
illusions produced by an old piece of 'magicke glasse'. He claimed to
have used it to put a curse on the Spanish Armada.

He is also notable for inventing the concept of the British Empire.
He was asked by the queen to establish the legal framework for
colonising North America. He based his argument on the discovery
of America by Prince Madog and the establishment of a Welsh
colony, which we looked at earlier. He developed his argument by
saying that King Arthur had conquered lands there, which you might
think was mere speculation.

He spent his time invoking spirits and interpreting their
messages. He put a lot of faith in a colleague, Edward Kelley, who

EDW.^D KELLY, A MAGICIAN.
in the Act of invoking the Spirit of a Deceased Person.

was not much more than a confidence trickster. Kelley claimed he
could turn copper into gold using a secret powder taken from a
bishop's tomb in Wales. During a conference with the angels whilst
they were in Bohemia in 1587, Kelly told Dee that they had been
ordered to share their wives. Dee was horrified but allowed the
arrangement to proceed, although the request effectively ended
any further communication with those pesky angels. His wife
Jane died of the plague in 1604 in Manchester, where Dee was
warden of Christ's College. Apparently he predicted the date of his
own death.

Rowland Lee, 1487–1543

Rowland Lee came from a Northumberland family but despite such a handicap had an enormous effect upon the history of Wales. You might get some idea of the sort of impact he had when you consider the reputation he had, as indicated by his (unofficial) title, 'the Hanging Bishop'.

He was Bishop of Coventry and Litchfield and a respected administrator and all-round establishment figure. He may have officiated at the marriage of Anne Boleyn and Henry VIII, and certainly helped in preparing the king's divorce proceeding against Catherine of Aragon. Lee was one of the first bishops to take the Oath of Supremacy, recognising Henry as the Supreme Head of the Church of England.

As a recognition of his devotion, Rowland Lee was rewarded in May 1534 with the position of Lord President of the Council of Wales and the Marches. His first job was to bring law and order to Wales. He didn't like the Welsh much. In fact, he was described as a 'great despiser of Welshmen', which, as far as he was concerned, was a raging compliment. Lee instituted a reign of considerable terror in his plan to bring Wales back into line. He convicted and executed relentlessly. He claimed to have hanged over 5,000 Welshmen in five years.

He seemed to operate on the principle that in the end it was better to hang too many rather than to miss a few. Once, it is said, he was so cross that a prisoner had cheated the gallows by dying in prison that he ordered the dead body to be hanged anyway.

He was proud of the title of 'the Hanging Bishop'. It suited him. Of course, the Act of Union in 1536 sent him into a rage. He was convinced that the Welsh could not be trusted in any circumstances.

Rowland Lee died in 1543 and is buried in St Chad's church in Shrewsbury. And you may be as interested as I was to learn that the motto of St Chad's is 'open doors, open hearts, and open minds' ...

The Act of Union in February 1536 stated that 'Wales was already incorporated, annexed, united and subject to and under the imperialle crowne of this realm as a very member of the same'. It was passed by an English parliament, with no Welsh representatives.

The Baron and the Red Bandits

Lewis Owen was a powerful man – one of the most influential men in North Wales. He was Sheriff of Merionethshire – the first Welshman to serve in this capacity – and became vice-chamberlain and baron for the whole area.

He took a vigorous approach to the suppression of local outlaws who roamed the area. They were numerous and especially bold. They had operated unchecked for some time, burning down houses and committing murder. A notorious and highly feared group were known as the Red Bandits of Mawddwy (they were allegedly distinguished by their red hair). It was said that farmers kept scythes hidden in their chimneys for their defence if the bandits came to call. They were so confident that they often stole herds of cattle and moved them about in broad daylight. Robert Vaughan, a local historian from Dolgellau, described them as acting without fear, shame, pity or punishment. This couldn't go on and Owen was determined to confront them. He recruited a group of tall and lusty men and raided the outlaws on Christmas Eve 1554, detaining eighty, whom they punished 'according to the nature of their delinquencies'. He was intent on bringing order and quiet government to North Wales, but he was to pay a high price.

Lewis Owen travelled to Montgomery to visit the Lord of Mawddwy in October 1555. His son was to marry the lord's daughter and there were plans to be made. On his way home the Red Bandits, a damned crew of thieves and outlaws, were waiting for him at Bwlch y Fedwen. They were a prosperous group who, up until now, had made a good living out of crime. Owen seemed to be derailing their business plan.

> ✦ There was a group of bandits who were called *Plant Mat*
> (Mat's Children) who lived in a cave near Devil's Bridge
> in Cardiganshire, from where they terrorised the local area
> until they were captured and executed. They were accused
> of murdering a judge at Rhyader and as a result the court of
> Great Sessions was transferred from there to Presteigne in 1542.

Owen was dragged from his horse and killed with spears and billhooks. His companions fled, apart from his son-in-law John Lloyd, who tried to defend him until he too was killed, with over thirty wounds to his body. Eight murderers were tracked down and executed, ending the power of the Red Bandits. It was such a shame that Owen paid for peace in Merionethshire with his own life.

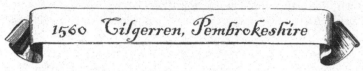

1560 Cilgerren, Pembrokeshire

The Boke of Chyldren

Thomas Phaer (1510–1560) was born in Norwich but work and marriage took him to Wales. He became Solicitor to the Council of the Marches and settled in Cilgerran. He married Anne, daughter of Alderman Thomas Walter of Carmarthen and became magistrate, customs searcher and Commissioner for Piracy.

He was a successful writer. He wrote legal works and was a highly regarded translator of Virgil's *Aeneid*. In 1559 he was awarded a Bachelor of Medicine degree from Oxford and then a doctorate, after having practiced medicine, by his own admission, for twenty years.

His greatest fame came from his medical works, written in English. The first was *A Goodly Bryefe Treatise of the Pestylence* but the greatest was *The Boke of Chyldren*. It was extremely popular, running to several editions until 1596. It contains forty conditions with 'remedyes' in each case, including 'bredyng of teeth' and 'pyssyng in bed'. The book recognises children as a special class of patients, often ones who cannot explain precisely their symptoms. He considers 'manye grievous and perilous diseases' in his book. So you will find references to 'apostume of the brayne' (meningitis) and terrible 'dreames and feare in the slepe' (nightmares). His book contains references to antibiotics made from mould, using the 'musherom called iewes eares'.

Phaer said parents should avoid elaborate and expensive cures. 'Of small pockes and measilles the best and most sure helpe in this case is not to meddle with anye kynde of medicines but to let nature work her operacion.' Wise – and cheap – advice.

Of course some of what he writes is rooted very much in the time that he lived and opens a fascinating window on his world. In this way it is a valuable record of social history. Whilst accidents in the home are as important now as they were then, few of us today would say that the major cause of ulceration of the head is from sides of bacon or salt beef falling from hooks in the ceiling.

Sadly it was an accident that stopped him writing. He fell from his horse in 1560 and injured his right hand, dying from complications.

✦ In 1551 Thomas Phaer surveyed the coast of Wales for Edward VI. He wrote 'all along this coast is no trade of merchandise but all full of rocks and danger.'

 1563 Llangamarch

A Drama in Disguise

John Penry was born at Cefn-brith at Llangamarch in 1563 and educated first at Peterhouse in Cambridge and then at Oxford. He became a well-known Puritan and religious agitator.

An Act of Parliament had made provision for translating the Bible into Welsh in 1562 and the New Testament had been issued in 1567; however, there weren't many copies. Penry was very concerned with the state of religious leadership and preaching in Wales. Many couldn't speak Welsh and congregations were shrinking. He described bishops as 'murderers and stranglers of men's souls' and clergymen as 'dumb and greedy dogs'. Forceful language, if a bit unwise.

He petitioned the queen in 1587 to improve things, but attacks on the Church were considered to be treasonable. He was imprisoned for a month and called 'a lewd boy' by the Archbishop of Canterbury, John Whitgift, who was not a man you could afford to upset. Puritans called Whitgift the 'Beelzebub of Canterbury'.

Penry disappeared to Scotland for a while in 1589 but on his return to London in 1593 he was arrested, accused of exciting rebellion and insurrection. He claimed that his single desire had only ever been to save the souls of the Welsh people. However, despite this laudable aim he was executed – a little hastily, some believe – in Surrey, on gallows erected on the road to Canterbury, late in the afternoon of 29 May 1593.

But there is more. The poet and dramatist Christopher Marlowe was allegedly killed the following day. Some believe that there is a conspiracy theory here; perhaps Marlowe was not killed at all. Penry's body was quickly taken the short distance to Deptford and passed off as Marlowe's to people who didn't know either of them anyway. This enabled Marlowe to escape and assume the identity of Shakespeare.

Pure speculation of course, but what is undeniable is the fact that his four daughters were called Comfort, Deliverance, Safety and Sure Hope.

Let him, who nought for mother cares
Learn, with stepmother, how he fares.

– Welsh proverb

- Inside the Howell's department store building in Cardiff there is a plaque which marks the spot where Rawlins White was burnt at the stake in March 1555. He refused to accept the authority of the Pope during the reign of Queen Mary.

- Henry VII brought up his eldest son Arthur as a Welsh speaker.

- William Davies was born in 1593 in North Wales and trained as a Catholic priest in Reims in France. He was sent in 1585 to work as a missionary in Wales. He set up a printing press and secretly produced *Y Drych Christianogawl* (*The Christian Mirror*). It is believed to be the first book physically printed in Wales and it was probably produced in a cave above the sea at Llandudno.

- As a result, he was arrested at Holyhead and imprisoned in Beaumaris, where he was hanged, drawn and quartered in July 1593. His cassock was preserved as a holy relic.

- The name penguin may have come from the Welsh *pen gwyn* (meaning 'white head'). The logbook of the *Golden Hind* contains a reference to a bird 'which the Welsh men name Pengwin' that was seen in the Strait of Magellan at the bottom of South America.

- William Barlow, Bishop of St David's from 1536–1548, tried to have the see moved to Carmarthen. He stripped the lead off the roof of his palace in St David's to pay for his daughters' marriages.

- Henry VIII's official antiquarian, John Leland, was fascinated by the cave on Worm's Head at the tip of the Gower Peninsular. He wrote that, 'there is a wonderfull hole at the poyant of Worme Heade, but few dare entre it, and men fable there that a dore within the spatius hole hathe been sene withe great nayles on it.' Leland believed that behind this door there was an underground passage leading to other caves near Llandybïe and Carreg Cennen Castle. Sadly it isn't true.

- William Salesbury was born in Conwy and became a leading Welsh scholar. He was one of the principal translators of the 1567 Welsh New Testament. In 1547 he had published *A Dictionary in Englyshe and Welshe, moche necessary to all suche Welshemen as wil spedly learne the Englyshe tongue.* It is still a much-needed volume.

1578 Penarth

Cost Me Noughte

John Callis was a notorious Welsh pirate, but not for him the easy temperatures and exotic life of plunder in the tropics. Instead Callis terrorised the Bristol Channel for a while. He was active from Cardiff to Haverfordwest, selling acquisitions in Laugharne and Carew. And there were lots of people around him who gave him protection and support in return for a small profit from his adventures.

He was born in Monmouthshire, though the date of birth is unclear. But whilst he may have started out as a haberdasher, strangely the exciting life of a pirate was more appealing. He became captain of the quaintly named *Cost Me Noughte* and was soon known as 'The Master of the English Channel'.

His base was Penarth and many locals were complicit in his activities, buying stolen goods at discount prices, a trade which I believe still survives in some parts of the area. Sir John Perrot, Vice-Admiral for South Wales, was involved. He was accused of not taking steps to apprehend him. Similarly, local magistrates would release anyone who was caught.

It was a source of great frustration to the government in London. The Spanish Ambassador wrote to the Privy Council, 'I am much annoyed at having to be always troubling you with the robberies of pirates'. He complained that there had never been any 'restitution of plundered goods'. It was brutal but it was tolerated, especially when it was politically expedient.

Callis was eventually arrested in 1578 and tried on ten counts of piracy. He did a deal to escape the gallows, revealing pirate hiding places and their supporters. He named the Sheriff of Glamorgan as an accomplice. Stories that he was hanged in Newport for piracy are probably untrue.

It seems that on his release he joined an expedition to the West Indies as a pilot but was soon back to his old trade. His new ship was *The Golden Chalice* but he realised that he was living on borrowed time, so he relocated his business to the Mediterranean. He was killed there in 1587.

In March 1573 the Privy Council instructed sheriffs and justices to reduce the number of alehouses in Wales because they contributed to lawlessness. They argued:

> … thieves, murderers and women of light conversation are harboured, rogues and vagabonds maintained, whoredom, filthy and detestable life much frequented, unlawful game as tables, dice, cards, bowls, quoits and such like commonly exercised, bows and arrows left outside to the great decay of artillery and emboldening and encouragement of the common enemy.

Sadly we still wrestle largely with the same issues today.

1594 Denbigh

On the Fly

Gwen had a reputation for healing and charming. She had been born in Llandyrnog in the Vale of Clwyd and was regarded as having a particular skill in making medicines for animals and general potions and ointments. She made no charge for her treatments, but accepted goods like butter and cheese in exchange.

She also admitted to using charms to assist the sick. People would travel to see her. Her charms seemed to involve asking God to protect and deliver the sick from the influence of the Evil One. It all seems rather innocent.

But she also used written charms, and these were her downfall. One was found in the parlour of Thomas Mostyn, a Justice of the Peace. The charm was a biblical quotation written backwards. This was believed to reverse the power of the Bible; no longer good, but evil.

Gwen had been unwittingly caught up in a quarrel between ex-lovers. It seems likely that the charm was planted in the Mostyn house by spurned lover Jane Conway, because Thomas owed her money.

Unfortunately, another written charm was found in her purse when she was searched. People came forward to denounce her. Some said that she would deliberately send people in the wrong direction when advising them where to look for their lost cattle. So she was condemned as a witch, either for getting it right or for getting it wrong. A visitor to her house said he had been given beer, on the surface of which was an abnormally large fly, clearly a projection of her evil spirit. The key accusation was that she had cursed Lewis Richards who became unstable and paranoid. He died because she refused to treat him. She was found guilty of murder by witchcraft.

She was hanged in the town square at Denbigh in June 1594, the first prosecution for witchcraft in north-east Wales.

LC-DIG-ppmsc-07409

> ✦ In 1597 there was a riot in Ffestiniog. The family and servants
> of the owner of a herd of cattle which had been stolen were
> attacked by the rustlers whilst trying to track them down.

 1607 *Bristol Channel*

The Great Deluge

It might well be one of the most important events in Welsh history
and, in some interpretations, the most alarming. And if those people
are right then it could happen again – and if it did … well, the consequences are almost unimaginable.

Let's go back to 1607 and consider the weather on 20 January. It is
the key to the 'Great Deluge', which swamped the Bristol Channel
and reshaped the coastline forever. You see, if the weather was dark
and wet then it was a storm surge, like the one which devastated the
Norfolk Broads in 1953. An unfortunate combination of weather
conditions centred upon a severe depression off the coast of Ireland
combined with a high tide which sent waves racing up the Channel.
As the waves were compressed by the narrowing shoreline, their speed
and height increased so that by the time they reached Chepstow they
are thought to have been 25ft high and travelling at almost 40mph.

The water spread far and wide. Cardiff was very badly damaged.
The foundations of St Mary's church were washed away. It is
estimated that along the Channel, from Laugharne to Chepstow,
over 2,000 people died in the country's worst ever natural disaster.
Houses and villages were swept away. Approximately 200 square
miles were inundated. Even Glastonbury – 14 miles inland – was
affected. Churches like St Mary's in Goldcliff have flood plaques,
indicating the level that the water reached.

But let's for a moment go back to the weather. If it was bright and
sunny on 20 January, as some contemporary reports suggest, then it
wasn't a storm surge at all. It was a tsunami. Those same reports talk
about the sea receding before it surged back, which is characteristic
of a tidal wave. And if that is the case then the 'Great Deluge' could
happen again, for there is a fault system in the Atlantic off the coast
of Ireland, waiting for another opportunity …

Of course, it is unlikely. But if it did happen, insurance claims are expected to exceed £12 billion – as long as the flood water didn't affect nuclear power stations on the Severn at Hinkley Point and Oldbury, that is …

At the time the 'Great Deluge', rather like the biblical flood, was seen as God's punishment for the sinful behaviour of the Welsh. You would have to say that things are not really a great deal better 400 years later. Let's hope He isn't ready to wipe the slate clean once more.

+ In 1607 there was a serious outbreak of plague in Conwy.

 ## 1612 Westminster

The Royal Swear Box

Henry Frederick, Prince of Wales, was the eldest son of King James I and a much-loved heir to the throne. He was regarded as a prince who would inspire and lead his country through his talents and popularity. His childhood had been disrupted, for he had been separated from his mother, Anne of Denmark, to protect him from her Catholic sympathies. Whether this had caused him any long-term emotional damage isn't clear, though he did develop his own fierce anti-Catholic opinions.

He was educated by a succession of notable tutors. It is said that James much preferred the role of schoolmaster to that of father, and certainly a distance developed between the king and his son. He was heir to the throne and yet appeared to have been starved of proper family relationships.

Henry went to Magdalen College in Oxford, where his reputation prospered to the extent that it threatened James' position. There were certainly tensions – on one occasion they almost came to blows during a hunt.

Henry Frederick features in our collection of Welsh strangeness because of his enthusiastic promotion of the Royal Swear Box. He fined all those who swore in his presence, insisting that they contribute to his alms box for the poor. The income generated is not recorded.

He was invested as Prince of Wales in 1610 but it was a privilege that he did not enjoy for long. Sadly he died of typhoid fever in November 1612 when he was only 18 years old. His death was regarded as a tragedy for the monarchy: a talented and popular prince taken before his time. At his funeral – which James refused to attend – a naked man ran through the mourners, shouting loudly that he was Henry's ghost.

The succession to the throne of England passed to his unpopular younger brother, who Henry had also disliked intensely. The brother became Charles I and in that moment the whole direction of English history was altered …

✦ In 1606 the Union Flag which represents the union between England and Scotland was created by royal decree. Wales is not represented in the design.

 1616 `Cambriol`

Times Change. Values Don't.

This was the name given to one of the first English colonies established in North America: Cambriol (meaning 'a little Wales'), founded by Sir William Vaughan. He bought land from The Company of Adventurers in Newfoundland in 1616 – and the reason you have never heard of it is because it disappeared.

Vaughan was born in Llangydeyrn in Carmarthenshire and was known as a dreamer, as well as being religious 'almost to the point of mania'. He was very concerned about conditions in Wales. All around him he saw poverty and a lack of ambition, people leading grim and uninspired lives. He decided that a fresh start was needed overseas. There should be a settlement which would inspire and revive the national spirit. He was looking for something similar to Nova Scotia founded by his friend Sir William Alexander, something that would generate wealth and provide entertainment for the rich, employment for the poor, advantage for adventurers. A bit like a contemporary theme park, I suppose. And Newfoundland was clearly the place – 'a country reserved by God for us Britons' (Sir William Vaughan, *The Golden Fleece*, 1626) – and possibly better than his original choice of St Helena. There were abundant natural resources and docile natives.

Once he had bought the land he recruited Welsh men and women to be the first colonists who departed in 1617. Vaughan didn't go with them. He was unwell.

He appointed Sir Richard Whitbourne as the first Governor, and he set off in 1618 in two ships to see how they were getting on. One ship carried provisions and the other was a fishing boat intended to work in the Newfoundland fishery. Sadly this boat was seized by pirates en route.

The disasters continued. Whitbourne discovered that the colonists were not really up to the job. He reported that they were 'such idle persons' who had done very little to create anything sustainable. He sent them home, apart from six who were told to build a house for Vaughan. Sir William finally turned up in 1622 but spent his time in the colony writing his book *The Golden Fleece* to inspire the colonists. He returned to England in order to publish it.

It was clear that he had never engaged with the reality of creating a viable settlement. He seriously misjudged the weather; the colonists were overwhelmed by Arctic conditions and ravaged by scurvy. Vaughan's response was to publish *The Newlander's Cure*, a book of self-help remedies.

Of course, the colony failed. Isolated and unsupported, it was abandoned sometime after 1630. Vaughan blamed the 'absence of the Ten Commandments to the west of Ireland', which was a bit unfair. The colonists were so poor that they didn't have anything to steal or indeed an ox to covet.

 1631 *Hudson Bay*

He Stoppeth One of Three

It is strange but some people believe it to be true that Coleridge's great poem, *The Rime of the Ancient Mariner*, was inspired by the (allegedly) Welsh sea captain, Thomas James (1593–1635).

In his time he was a respected navigator and explorer who set
out from Bristol in May 1631 on the *Henrietta Maria* in search of
the north-west passage to Asia around the top of America. It was
a voyage of exceptional hardships. He explored the west coast
of James Bay, naming it after himself and scattering other names
everywhere. He called one place 'Cape Monmouth'. The southern
coast he named 'The New Principality of South Wales' and a large
river the 'New Severn'. He chose Charlton Island as the place to
see out the winter. They built several shelters and took off their
supplies. On 29 November he deliberately sank the *Henrietta Maria*
to prevent her from being crushed by ice or blown away.

The intention was either to refloat her or rebuild her. However his choices were considerably reduced when the ship's carpenter was one of the six men who died over the winter. In June 1632 the ship was refloated and drained. The rudder was rehung and he set sail for home on 1 July. It took three weeks to get through the ice in James Bay and the crew believed it a daily miracle that it did not sink. The ship finally reached Bristol on 22 October 1632, barely afloat.

He wrote a best-selling book of his near-death experiences and of a crew tortured by scurvy and intense cold. He wrote that 'many complained of infirmities, some of sore mouths, all the teeth in their heads being loose, their gums swolne, with blacke rotten flesh, which must every day be cut away'.

The book could have provided Coleridge with important material. After all, in his poem, he writes: 'The ice was here, the ice was there / The ice was all around'.

James' next command was the *9th Whelp of the Lion* and he spent his last years patrolling the Bristol Channel suppressing piracy.

 1635 Llanrhymney

Henry Morgan

Henry Morgan was many things, but technically he wasn't a pirate. He brought death and mayhem to all parts of the Caribbean, but he preferred to be known as an admiral and a privateer.

First of all, what was a privateer? Someone with, in his case, a licence issued by the Governor of Jamaica instructing him to fight the Spanish wherever he could find them. His pay was essentially whatever he could steal. So like a pirate, but legal.

Henry Morgan was born in Llanrhymney, near Tredegar, and it isn't clear how he ended up in the Caribbean. He might have been 'Barbadosed' (knocked unconscious on the docks in Bristol and taken away to become a labourer) – an interesting recruitment technique that some call centres have tried to revive. Alternatively he joined the army in Plymouth and was sent to fight the Spanish in the West Indies. Either way, he became part of General Venables' ill-fated army that in 1658 was defeated and retreated to Jamaica.

- In 1623 two sisters and their brother were hanged in Caernarfonshire for bewitching Margaret Hughes and laming her sister.

- Oliver Cromwell (1599–1648) was descended from Morgan Williams of Llanishen in Cardiff, who was a brewer and innkeeper. Others believe that Oliver Cromwell was born on the Margam Abbey Estate.

- During the Civil War the tomb of Marmaduke Lloyd at St David's Cathedral was desecrated. Three images attached to the tomb were removed and their heads knocked off. For a laugh one of the Parliamentarian supporters took one of the images to the font in order to christen it. Unfortunately he dropped it on his foot. His toe was injured, causing him to develop gangrene, which soon killed him.

- William Vaughan was granted the position of General of Horse for Wales and the Borders by Charles I in 1645. However, his troopers acquired 'an evil name' when they were involved in pillaging Dolgellau's drapers. Vaughan himself was killed in 1649.

- The news of the defeat of the Royalist army at Rowton Moor in September 1645 was delivered to King Charles in Chester by Colonel Shakerley, who crossed the River Dee in a tub.

- Humffrey Jones of Penrhyn (near Bangor) served as the King's Receiver. As a Royalist, his home was raided by Parliamentarians in 1645. He invited the intruders to sample the contents of his extensive cellar. Whilst they were thus relaxed, Royalist forces were summoned, who captured thirty-six Parliamentary soldiers.

- During the Civil War (in around 1648), Swansea was said to have surrendered three times in one day. The town started off the day as a Royalist town, but during the morning surrendered to a small detachment of Cromwell's army. By the afternoon the King's Army returned and retook the town. In the evening Cromwell himself arrived and addressed his soldiers on the sands. They recited a prayer and a hymn and he spoke firmly to the town. They surrendered again. So whilst the Parliamentarians marched in through the Mount Gate, the Royalists left through the Greenhill gate at the top of the town.

But of course it was at sea that he made his reputation. By 1661 he was commanding his own ship and he was soon feared as an uncompromising and ruthless privateer. Henry Morgan was regarded as the worst enemy of Spain since Sir Francis Drake. He used the wealth he accumulated to establish sugar plantations – which were based of course upon the death and torture of hundreds of innocents.

As relations between England and Spain fluctuated, so did Morgan's position. Often he was useful in exercising naval power and authority. When relationships improved he was an embarrassment and on one occasion arrested, since he threatened a fragile peace. He spent about two years in London as a celebrity, dining out on stories of his exploits and advising on improvements to the defences of Jamaica. Then in 1675 he was useful again. He was knighted and sent back to Jamaica as Lieutenant Governor.

Morgan died there, possibly of alcohol poisoning, in August 1688. He was buried in an elaborate ceremony in the Palisadoes cemetery in Port Royal in Jamaica. The cemetery disappeared beneath the sea in an earthquake in 1692; divine retribution for the sinful ways of its occupants.

 1649 Covent Garden

A Golden Ticket?

John Poyer is a neglected character from the English Civil War – and his unfortunate death should serve as a warning to anyone who has ever considered buying a raffle ticket. Winning isn't everything.

Poyer was Mayor of Pembroke and initially a devoted supporter of the Parliamentary cause during the English Civil War. Whilst all of South Wales was entirely of Royalist persuasion, Tenby and Pembroke were not. Poyer plotted and schemed to maintain his position. He refused to step down at the end of his term of office in 1642, since his successor was a Royalist.

Poyer was a considerable inconvenience to Royalists – they promised that they would roll him down into the sea inside a barrel pierced by nails, which perhaps indicates a certain level of irritation with him. But the Civil War ended in 1646 with Poyer on the victorious side. However, he was called to London to face charges of misappropriating land and property, and while the charges were not pursued, he was deeply offended that the Parliamentary cause for which he had fought had chosen to question his actions.

The war might have been won but the country was full of unpaid soldiers, waiting for their back pay. When Poyer was ordered to give up control of Pembroke he refused, saying that he would vacate only when the wages had been settled.

The country slumped back into war – with Poyer now declaring his support for the king. A large Parliamentary force under General Horton advanced into Wales and defeated Poyer easily at the Battle of St Fagans on 4 May 1648, the last battle to be fought in Wales. Poyer retreated to Pembroke where he surrendered after a brief siege in July 1648.

At a military court in April 1649, Poyer and two colleagues were found guilty of treason and condemned to death. However, the Council of State decided, rather bizarrely, that only one of the three should die. The decision would be determined by a child, who would draw lots to decide who should face the firing squad. The winning ticket belonged to Poyer, who was executed in Covent Garden on 25 April 1649.

John Poyer, chosen for death by a lottery arranged by Puritan authorities who rejected any form of gambling … unlucky.

1660 *Maesygarnedd*

Death Warrant

As you will know, there have always been many men in Wales called John Jones. This is why this particular one is often identified by the addition of his home, Maesygarnedd.

But really, there is no need. There is something far more notorious that distinguishes him from all others. For John Jones of Maesygarnedd was one of the men who signed the death warrant for Charles I. John Jones was, in fact, a regicide.

He was born in Llanbedr in North Wales and lived at Maesygarnedd in Merionethshire. While Wales was generally a country of Royalist sympathisers, he was an ardent supporter of the Parliamentary cause – and because of this was described by his contemporaries as 'the most hated man in North Wales'. Quite an achievement.

By 1646 he was a colonel in the army and highly regarded as a diligent and trustworthy colleague. He was selected as a judge at the trial of Charles I and was one of the signatories of the death warrant. He married Oliver Cromwell's sister and served as Governor of Anglesey.

He did not seem to recognise that he was in considerable danger when the monarchy was restored. Jones made no attempt to escape; he was arrested in Finsbury and imprisoned in the Tower of London in June 1660. He was tried in October when he admitted quite freely the part that he had played. He was found guilty and was hanged, drawn and quartered on 17 October 1660, one of the ten regicides executed in that month at either Tyburn or Charing Cross. Apparently, he met his death with great dignity.

- Judge Jeffreys, the notorious 'Hanging Judge' at the Bloody Assizes following the Monmouth Rebellion in 1685, was born at Acton Hall at Wrexham in 1645.

- By 1660, 108 books had been published in Welsh.

- Thomas Myddelton, who died in 1631, was the son of the Governor of Denbighshire and financed the publication of a Welsh-language Bible. He made his fortune in trade, having been apprenticed as a young man to a grocer in London.

- In 1646 the island of Skokholm was bought by William Phillips, a barrister. His descendants retained ownership for 300 years.

- Elihu Yale (1649–1721) was born in Connecticut but came to Wales as a child. He joined the East India Company in Madras in 1670 and became governor of the company from 1688 to 1699. He retired to Wrexham as an extremely wealthy man and became an influential benefactor of local causes. It was his gift of books, pictures and, most importantly, money to a college in New Haven in America that gave him immortality. In 1745 the college took his name and became Yale University. Elihu Yale is buried in St Giles' churchyard in Wrexham.

There is in fact a regicide who is buried in Wales: Henry Marten from Oxfordshire who died imprisoned in Chepstow Castle. Marten was a great survivor. Not for him the horror of public execution. Rather a comfortable imprisonment in well-appointed rooms in Marten's Tower, with every opportunity for reviving walks around the town followed by dinner parties with local notables.

Marten had helped to draft the charges brought against the king and to organise the trial. His particular claim to fame is that during the signing of the death warrant, he and Cromwell flicked blobs of ink at each other. His death penalty was commuted probably because, as a contrary and contradictory man, he'd protected Royalists during the 1650s. Marten died in September 1680, choking whilst eating his supper. You can find his tombstone hidden under a carpet in the entrance to St Mary's church in Chepstow.

Davy Morgan – Celebrity Master Thief

Born in Brecon in 1669, Morgan went to London to work as a serving man to an unidentified Welsh knight in 1687. He soon learned that he could earn more money by selling his master's clothes and stealing his money. So Davy disappeared into a life of crime and embraced

a career as a burglar, a shoplifter and a pickpocket. His first notable job was when he broke into the house of the Venetian Ambassador in Pall Mall and took £200 worth of silver plate. He was detained and imprisoned.

On his release he led a gang that broke into the home of Titus Oates in Axe Yard, Westminster. Oates had invented the Popish Plot, an entirely spurious conspiracy theory suggesting that King Charles II was an assassination target. At least fifteen innocent men had been executed. Such behaviour was clearly offensive to Davy's ethical code. Whilst his colleagues ransacked the house, Davy trussed up Titus Oates and gagged him, saying that if he had been prevented from speaking sooner, he would not have 'sworn so many men's lives away for pastime'.

Davy developed a taste for celebrities. He robbed Bully Dawson, a famous London gambler. He called on him in a gaming house, when he had won a great deal of money. Davy took 18 guineas from him at gunpoint, tied him up and fled. To be honest he seems to have a thing about tying up celebrities, a service which he offered free of charge.

He committed a particularly lucrative robbery from a Jewish family in London and fled to Wales with over £2,000 in gold. In Presteigne he stole the communion plate from the parish church and then broke into the house of Edward Williams. Sadly it went horribly wrong and Williams was murdered.

Davy Morgan was arrested in Bristol and executed in Presteigne in April 1712 at the age of 43. His body was hanged in chains. His ex-lover came to view the body and is alleged to have said, 'Poor Davy, how sadly art though exposed to all the felicities of wind and weather.' An ignominious end, even for a man untroubled by the concept of celebrity.

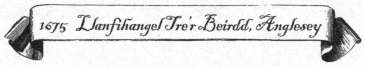

1675 Llanfihangel Tre'r Beirdd, Anglesey

Difficult Sums

There have been so many Welshmen called William Jones, and so many who fit this description – 'a little short-faced Welshman who used to treat his mathematical friends with a great deal of roughness and freedom'. It is a tough life, being a mathematical friend sometimes.

And his chums were significant ones – Sir Isaac Newton, Sir Edmund Halley – and the story of this great mathematician begins in Anglesey. The mathematical ability of William Jones (1675–1749) was quickly identified, for it went far beyond that of the people around him who, like the rest of us, were still struggling with the concepts of adding up and taking away. He was given a job at a London counting house by the local landowner, Lord Bulkeley. Jones was soon serving in the navy, first in the West Indies and then as a teacher of navigation. He was a private tutor to the famous, basing himself in coffee shops. In 1711 he used Child's Coffee House in St Paul's churchyard as his address. For a small fee customers would pay to listen to him lecture, which boosted business in the same way as a satellite sports channel today.

In 1706 he published *Synopsis Palmanorium Matheseo*, a work of theorems on differential calculus and infinite series, intended apparently for the beginner. Sadly this beginner can't get beyond the title. But this book introduced pi as a mathematical symbol, because as he said, the exact proportion between the diameter and the circumference can never be expressed in numbers, so a symbol was needed to represent it.

William Jones was Vice-President of the Royal Society and he accumulated a vast library of over 15,000 books. It was regarded as the most valuable library of mathematics in the world at that time.

He died in 1749 of a 'polypus in the heart' and is buried in St Paul's.

1681 Presteigne

Hot Spots

Like a number of small towns across England and Wales, Presteigne was saved from the plague by one of those outbreaks of fire that always threatened closely packed timber-framed buildings and their thatched roofs. But in retrospect it wasn't entirely bad news. The cleansing properties of destruction should never be dismissed.

In Presteigne, fire broke out on the night of 12 September 1681. Over sixty houses in the High Street and in St David's Street were completely destroyed as fire ripped through the wattle and daub and the timber frames and scoured the ruins clean of disease and infection. Apparently only one resident died in the fire – a blind woman. The fire also destroyed the 'schoole and schoolehouse' which had been founded by John Beddoes in 1565 opposite the church.

Apparently such was the sympathy generated by the devastating fire that in March 1682 the people of Topsham in Devon collected 11s 5½d as a donation for 'those in Presteigne in Wales who suffred by fire', which was extremely generous.

There was a similar fire in Builth almost ten years later in 1690 when approximately forty houses were destroyed in a fire. The fire is believed to have raged for five hours, resulting in more than £12,000 worth of damage. The people of Builth were permitted by the Crown to seek financial assistance from those who were prepared to make a charitable donation.

However, while they managed to receive far more than the fine people of Presteigne, somehow it just wasn't quite enough. Notwithstanding the fact that at least £100 was collected, which puts them a long way ahead of Presteigne in the compassion stakes, it just wasn't enough for their needs. Only one house was actually rebuilt from this fund – which is probably the building now known as the White Horse Hotel. It is likely that the inhabitants of Builth, pragmatic as always, did not wait for the charity of distant towns and villages. They preferred to use stones taken from the ruined and redundant castle as building material for their damaged town.

+ In 1682 the Court of The Great Sessions in Bala threatened to burn Quakers. This prompted the Welsh Quakers to acquire land around what was later called Pennsylvania, where they emigrated.

 1682 Casnewydd Bach

Black Bart – Pirate of the Caribbean

Be proud. Black Bart, the most successful pirate of his generation, capturing over 470 vessels, was one of our own. He was either a teetotal fancy-man who was nice to ladies or, alternatively, he was

a psychotic killer. For a while he was the most feared man in the Caribbean, dangerous and unpredictable.

He was probably born in Casnewydd Bach in Pembrokeshire in 1682. His real name was John Roberts and after joining the crew of the pirate ship *The Rover* following his capture at sea, he embarked on his new career with impressive enthusiasm. He changed his name to Bartholomew and soon Black Bart was captain himself and being hunted down for his crimes. He didn't much like it.

In late February 1720 he was attacked by two ships from Barbados, and soon two vessels from Martinique were hunting for him. He had a new flag made with a drawing of himself standing upon two skulls, one labelled ABH ('A Barbadian Head') and the other AMH ('A Martiniquian Head'). You always knew where you stood with Bart. His flag was an important design concept – a forerunner of the infamous Jolly Roger.

When they captured a French man-of-war and discovered that one of the passengers was the Governor of Martinique, he was hanged from the yardarm. They sailed on, spreading fear and destruction wherever they went.

By the spring of 1721, Black Bart had almost brought sea-borne trade in the West Indies to a standstill. But this was not good for business. There were no ships to plunder. Bart was forced to relocate to the coast of West Africa to seek out new business opportunities in an emerging market.

But it didn't work out. He was trapped and killed by Captain Chaloner Ogle on 10 February 1722.

1685 Rudbaxton

The Howard Memorial

In St Michael's church in Rudbaxton in Pembrokeshire there is a remarkable tomb. It takes up the whole of the side of the Lady chapel and commemorated members of the Howard family. Five of them stand there like brightly coloured dolls, four of them holding skulls. It is a rather macabre design. The figures are dressed in Restoration style in grey and red, apart from Joanna, in the middle. She is the 'woman in black', the one who is not holding a skull. She does have something in her hand but no one has managed to identify what it is. Might be dust, might be pebbles. But since she was responsible for the memorial (along with her daughter Mary Tasker) and wasn't dead at the time, perhaps a skull was felt to be inappropriate. She had it installed around 1685 as a parting gift for family and friends. I can only imagine how touched and impressed they were.

George, on the left, died in 1665 at the age of 32 and eagerly confirms this by pointing at the skull he is holding in his left hand. James and Joanna, probably his brother and sister-in-law, are in the centre and to the right their children, Thomas and Mary. Thomas sat briefly in Parliament until he was killed in a duel on 7 July 1682. In a final theatrical flourish, the figure of Thomas carries a clear red stain on the chest to represent his fatal duelling wound.

+ In 1685 the Quaker Thomas Briggs walked naked through Cardiff to promote the virtues of simplicity.

+ By an Act of 1687, those in receipt of poor relief were obliged to wear on their right sleeve a badge with a large 'P' for 'pauper' and the initial of the parish from which they came in red or blue.

 1693 London

On the Town

Reece Powel went out drinking with his mates in London in April 1693. It is what the Welsh have always done when they've gone up on a day trip. Reece was in town to deliver some accounts to the Excise Office and when that job was done, they all went to Edward Turner's public house. Perhaps they had a little more than they intended, because when they returned to their lodgings in Parker Lane they took with them one of Mr Turner's special silver tankards. I am sure they were not the first Welshmen to have walked off with

+ In December 1693, Maurice Jones of Egryn in Meirionethshire wrote of great balls of fire in the sky flying across the sea. In so doing, he became one of the first Welshmen to write about UFOs:

A fiery exhalation came from the sea and set fire to the hay with a blue weak flame. The fire, though easily extinguished, did not the least harm to any of the men who interposed their endeavour to save the hay, though they ventured (perceiving it different from common fire) not only close to it, but sometimes into it. (*Philosophical Transactions of Cambden's Brittania*) a beer mug from a London pub and they were certainly not the last, but the authorities looked upon such things differently in those days. The tankard was found in the possession of Reece Powel. He said that he knew nothing about it and that one of the others must have taken it, but that cut little ice. He was found guilty and sentenced to a period of service in the navy.

1701 Chepstow

David Roberts – Golden Boy

It is hard to consider David Roberts as one of Chepstow's finest because, as the judge noted when he condemned him, Roberts didn't rob one person. By filing bits off guineas he was committing a crime against the whole nation. And so he was hanged at Tyburn in August 1739. He was 38.

He'd been born in 1701 in Chepstow and eventually became apprenticed to a carpenter. He moved to Devizes where he lodged in the White Hart Inn and married the landlord's daughter. They had two children but she died in labour. Having squandered her dowry, Roberts took off for London. He lodged in another inn, this time run by a widow. The Old Bailey records tell us that 'he soon became so intimate with her that she told him it was necessary he should marry her'. Fair enough you might think, but in marrying her he inherited her debts and he got fed up with being arrested for

non-payment so he sold the household furniture and left her. But he couldn't escape.

He became involved with Sarah Bristow, who had been transported but had illegally returned. They moved first to Bristol and then to Coventry, but the creditors kept coming after him. His discovery of Sarah 'in a high degree of intimacy' with a friend called Carter doesn't appear to have bothered him too much, because it was Carter who taught him 'diminishing the coinage'. When Roberts filled a box with gold dust carefully filed off the edges, Sarah ran off with it so he got a new box, refilled it with more dust and employed someone at half a crown a day to sell it. They stole it too.

He escaped arrest by fleeing to Ramsgate with Sarah and her brother. They took a ferry to the Continent but quarrelled with the captain. Roberts threw the captain overboard but he was rescued while Roberts himself sailed the ferry to Calais. He escaped the customs men and fled back to London, where he started filing coins again. He was eventually arrested when Carter spotted him and reported him to the authorities … what a narrative.

And would it surprise you to learn that the night before his execution he confessed to murdering his first wife? No, I thought it wouldn't.

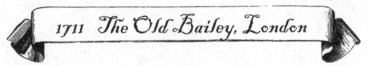

1711 The Old Bailey, London

Hair Today, Gone Tomorrow

Poor John Matthews. Sentenced to death at the Old Bailey in 1711. And all because of hair.

John Matthews, from Glamorgan, was convicted of stealing 24oz of hair from Mr Trott's barber shop and two wigs from Mr Newth in London. It was an open and shut case. Theft was theft, no matter how bizarre it might seem. Everyone knew he'd done it. He admitted it too. And the verdict was inevitable.

As he told the clergyman who attended to him between his trial and his execution, life hadn't always been so cruel. Matthews was 28 years old and he had come from a good family. He had tried always to live like a gentleman, but of course that was always so difficult. And always so expensive. Times were hard and so he had been reduced to making a living out of stealing from barber's shops.

He said that 'his urgent necessities forced him to do it.' Clearly he had found his own particular niche, though I am sure that in his own mind it was a case of how far the (imaginary) mighty had fallen. And now he knew that the only thing that awaited him was the noose.

This was the third occasion he'd been in court for the offence of stealing from barbers and he realised 'that he could not reasonably expect to find again that Mercy in this world which he formally had so much abused'. He knew that he was doomed.

So it proved.

On the day of the execution he spoke briefly to the crowd that had gathered at Tyburn for the entertainment to be provided by his death. He told them all to 'take warning by me'. He cried bitterly once he was placed upon the open cart and the rope was placed around his neck. As the cart began to move and he was about to fall off the end he screamed loudly.

'Lord have mercy upon me! Lord Jesu help me! Lord, haste thee unto me! Lord Jesu receive me!' (*The Proceedings of the Old Bailey*)

And all for a bag of someone else's hair.

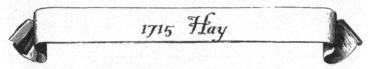

1715 Hay

George Price, 'with Hell in his Bosom'

George Price was born in Hay in 1715 and began his working life as a foot boy to a widow in Brecon, though it was suggested by some that he attended to more than her feet. He moved to London and met Mary Chambers, a fellow servant at a public house at Hampstead. Within two weeks they were married.

But he soon tired of her. He was not suited to family life and responsibility. As the court records said, 'he paid his addresses to other women'. The birth of twin daughters was a complication.

He persuaded Mary to kill the twins, by giving each of them three teaspoons of laudanum. It was, he said, a solution to their poverty. But Mary was pregnant again, which surprised him, 'with my enjoying you but once'. This was another problem to be dealt with. So he wrote to her: 'My dear, if you love me, do all these things that I desire you.' And what he desired was that she should take the 'stuff' that he sent her wrapped in a shirt. Boiled up with milk, it would induce a termination.

But Mary remained an obstruction to his happiness in his eyes. He told her he had found her a position as a nursery maid in Putney and that he would take her there in a chaise. Mary asked him to stop for some snuff. He refused and only stopped the chaise on

Houslow Heath, where he attacked her with his whip. He wrapped it around her neck and strangled her, pulling so hard that the handle broke. He reported that her last words were 'If this is your love, I will never trust you more'.

He stripped her body and left it beneath a gibbet, where two executed criminals were hanging in chains. He inexpertly tried to disfigure her by splitting her nose and cutting her face. He then dumped her clothes in different streets across London.

People were concerned at the disappearance of Mary and George fled to Portsmouth, Oxford, Hay and then Gloucester. He eventually returned to London where he surrendered himself. He was tried and condemned to death but he caught gaol fever and died before his execution in 1738 – 'one of the most notorious and execrable murderers who has at any time been heard of'. (*The Newgate Calendar*)

 1716 *Welshpool*

Cross Dressing

Let's be honest. You have probably always asked yourself, 'What is Welshpool's claim to fame?' Not an unreasonable question, and in fact there are two. The first is that it is the location of the largest sheep market in Europe.

Heady stuff, and more than enough, you might think. But there is more. There is the escape from execution in the Tower of London by Lord Nithsdale in 1716.

You see, this is all about the Jacobite rebellion, an attempt by James Stuart to restore the Stuart family to the throne and replace the Hanoverians. The unsuccessful outcome left three lords from Scotland facing execution in the Tower of London, one of whom was William Maxwell, Lord Nithsdale.

His wife, Lady Winifred, was a daughter of the Duke of Powis and was a little disappointed at the news of her husband's imminent beheading. So she hatched a plan which involved her visiting him in the Tower and then smuggling him out in woman's clothes, disguised as an overweight servant.

She travelled through the winter snow from Dumfries, with Grace Evans from Welshpool, her nurse since childhood. In London they

By kind permission of the Nithsdale family

then recruited the help of their landlady in Drury Lane, the large and possibly pregnant Mrs Mills.

On her tear-jerking visit to the Tower, Winifred dressed her husband, dyed his eyebrows, tied false ringlets in his hair and covered his beard in white powder. He buried his face in sorrow in a handkerchief and the guards unwittingly escorted him out of the Tower. How Mrs Mills felt about staying behind in his place is not recorded.

Nithsdale escaped to Lille, where he was reunited with Winifred and they lived out their years together in Rome. And Grace Evans' reward for her loyalty and support? A fine black-and-white cottage with brick gable stacks next to the church in Welshpool. It is now deservedly a listed building.

1732 Llanwrtyd Wells

Frog Spawned

Llanwrtyd Wells claims to be the smallest town in Britain, though how proud a boast that might be remains uncertain. Its fame as a medicinal spa started in 1732 when the local vicar, the Revd Theophilus Evans, watched a frog swimming in the waters of the local spring – Ffynnon Ddrewllyd – which translates rather attractively as 'stinking stream'. Not surprising really, since it contained sulphur. The brave vicar decided, rather strangely, that he had the same properties as a frog and tried the waters himself. He found that he was miraculously cured of scurvy. You might think that an invigorating drop of lime juice might be more palatable, but the swim certainly brought about considerable economic benefits to the town.

It established Llanwrtyd Wells as an important spa resort. When visitors first started to arrive the town was completely undeveloped. Houses had clay walls and roofs made of straw and rushes. The River Irfon was crossed by a very dodgy wooden bridge in constant need of repair. The strange compulsion to immerse yourself in pungent waters together with complete strangers transformed the town. For a long time the worried (and wealthy) arrived in their horse-drawn coaches. The clientele grew further with the arrival of the railway. The clean fresh air of mid-Wales and healthy companionship was attractive to those from the industrial regions. Throughout the history of the spa, visitors were generally Welsh-speaking and established their own entertainment with summer schools and concerts in the town.

Today there is different entertainment. Beer festivals, bog-snorkelling championships, a man versus horse marathon. The tourist office now describes Llanwrytd Wells as a 'world of wacky weird and wonderful outdoor activities'.

And all because of a frog.

+ In Strata Florida there is a gravestone that commemorates the left leg of Henry Hughes which was buried there on 18 June 1756. Henry lost his leg in a farming accident and emigrated to America, where the rest of him was eventually buried.

+ Sir Richard Steele, dramatist, politician and founder of *The Spectator* magazine was buried in St Peter's parish church, Carmarthen, in 1789. He met his second wife, Mary Scurlock from Llangunnor, at his first wife's funeral. He lived for a number of years in what is now the Ivy Bush Hotel in Carmarthen.

+ Daines Barrington (1727–1800) was a judge in Wales who encouraged archaeological research and scientific study. However, in England he was known as 'Daines, a man denied by nature Brains'.

+ William Jones (1746–1794), the son of William Jones – the great mathematician we met earlier – in a typical act of teenage rebellion, rejected maths in favour of linguistics. He established links between Greek, Latin and Sanskrit. He wrote in Persian under the pseudonym Youns Uksfardi, meaning 'Jones from Oxford'.

+ Sir John Pryce of Newtown Hall died in 1761. He kept the embalmed bodies of his first two wives on either side of his bed until his third wife insisted that they were removed.

+ In 1770, Carmarthen was the largest town in Wales, with 4,000 inhabitants.

+ William Pughe (1759–1835), writer and lexicographer, tried to prove that Welsh was closely related to the first human language.

+ The French philosopher and writer Voltaire sailed from Newport in 1729 after spending some time in exile in England. He said that he would retain Newport as a last pleasant memory of his stay in the country.

1736 Barry Island

Brandy for Barry

A report into smuggling in the Cardiff area was prepared by the Surveyor-General Thomas Ja'ans in 1736. He described Barry Island as 'a most hazardous district over-run by ruffians'.

Smuggling was commonplace. The officers employed to prevent it were incapable. One was 'old and infirm' and another 'spent more time in the tavern'.

Thomas Ja'ans decided things had to change. He left them with precise instructions about how to proceed, indicating where goods were often hidden – inside false bulkheads and decks, secret compartments in cabins and hollow masts, and deep in the middle of the ballast.

The seizure record did improve for a time and they were successful in identifying a smuggling operation which was landing brandy at Barry. The smugglers, however, escaped, apart from one, Thomas Isaak, who was arrested with a full and incriminating cask. However, he was conveniently regarded as an 'idiot who didn't know what he was doing' by a local jury and released.

1739 Nash Point

Pye-Eyed

In 1739 the *Pye*, a ship heading for Bristol carrying tobacco, sugar and cotton was wrecked off Nash Point in the Bristol Channel. People swarmed to the scene from all over the area. Estimates suggested there were over 300 people there helping themselves, and they easily drove away the small handful of customs officers sent to police the wreck.

Consequently, soldiers from Swansea were called in order to arrest the very worst gang at the scene. This was a vicious gang of shoemakers from Bridgend, apparently. However, the soldiers were unwilling to risk such a hazardous mission without a £20 bonus for each trooper. By the time these negotiations had been resolved, the cargo had disappeared.

Wrecked

During the day they were respected tradesmen – farmers, weavers and their wives. But at night they waited for the harvest from the sea. These were the feared Wreckers of Crigyll, who were always happy to supplement their pension plan by helping themselves to whatever washed ashore.

And on New Year's Eve 1740 they were in luck. The ship *Loveday and Betty* from Liverpool was driven ashore at Rhosneigr in Anglesey and the wreckers from nearby Crigyll saw a chance to start the New Year with a very welcome bonus. When the captain went off to get help, they stripped the ship of all that they could carry: sails, hawsers and pump handles. The three owners from Liverpool were understandably irritated by the loss of their property and they sought a prosecution.

Eventually six men were brought to trial in Beaumaris for 'plundering a shipwreck'. Owen Ambrose, two brothers called Hughes and three brothers called Roberts appeared before Mr Justice Martyn. The local merchants and traders gathered to see justice done, for their livelihoods had often been disrupted by the behaviour of the wreckers. But they had not reckoned with Mr Justice Martyn. He had a well-deserved reputation for drunkenness and incompetence and on this occasion he was at the very top of his game.

He drank prodigiously throughout his time in Beaumaris and deferred all court business until the last day of the session. Then he arbitrarily discharged all prisoners, who were released.

Locals were horrified. He had effectively given the wreckers a licence to continue their plunder and they continued to do so for another thirty years or so.

So incensed was Lewis Morris, the customs officer at Holyhead, that he wrote a poem about Crigyll:

> Where evil lives in the hearts of men,
> Bandits of the waves, vicious villains
> Hiding their lanterns under their cloaks.
> May God keep innocent travellers
> From wrecking on the rocks of Crigyll

- In May 1741 Thomas Williams, also known as Thomas Holloway, a labourer from Llangyndeyrn in Carmarthenshire, was prosecuted for highway robbery. He and his accomplice blackened their faces and ambushed Jane Harry. They took her money but returned 6½d so that she could drink to their health. Notwithstanding such fine and witty conduct, Williams was found guilty and sentenced to death. The accomplice disappeared.

- In April 1758 Mary Jones was brought to court in Cowbridge. She was accused of being a 'notorious vagrant' who had falsely claimed she was married to William Jones, a cooper in Swansea. She was found guilty. Mary was stripped above the waist and publicly whipped from the east gate of Cowbridge through the town to the west gate.

1773 Rhosneigr

On the Beach

Here we are again, back with our old friends, the Wreckers of Crigyll. It is strange but true that the only recorded example of a successful prosecution of wreckers who used false lights to lure ships on to the rocks happened as a result of an incident on an Anglesey beach.

In 1774 it was reported in the *Shrewsbury Chronicle* that Captain Chilcote brought charges against the 'opulent inhabitants of Anglesey' for 'plundering, stealing and taking away' casks of rum.

The wreckers were out on the beach shining lights into the darkness over the sea during a storm, trying to simulate the lights of Holyhead. On this occasion they lured in the ship the *Charming Jenny* from Tenby. Three crew members were killed when the vessel hit the rocks and Captain Chilcote and his wife managed to reach the shore on a makeshift raft. They lay exhausted on the beach. When the good captain recovered, he saw his wife lying dead close by. She had been stripped of most of her clothes. The pockets of her gown had been cut off and lay empty on the sand. They had once contained 70 guineas and the captain's watch. Her finger had been broken during the removal of her wedding ring.

Captain Chilcote had so far been untroubled, but as he lay there a man approached and cut the silver buckles from the shoes on his feet. Soon a large group of people turned up with carts and horses and disappeared into the night with his cargo of rum.

There have always been those who have believed that Mrs Chilcote's head had been held under the waves until she drowned. The captain was one of them and naturally he wanted revenge. Some of the wreckers were tried in Anglesey but they fought amongst themselves in the dock and were dismissed. Eventually in April 1774 they came to court in Shrewsbury. Two of the wreckers were sentenced to death. One had his sentence commuted to transportation and the other, Sion Parry, was hanged.

1776 United States of America

The Declaration of Independence

The Welsh are all over the early political history of America like a rash, following the settlement of many Welsh immigrants in Pennsylvania. The name Pennsylvania may not in fact come from the name of William Penn. He suggested that it came from the Welsh word *pen* meaning head, and that therefore it means head or high woodland.

There is a plaque on the wall of Philadelphia City Hall perpetuating the Welsh heritage and commemorating the vision and virtue of the following Welsh patriots in the founding of the City, Commonwealth and Nation. The plaque goes on to list William Penn, Thomas Jefferson, Robert Morris, Gouverneur Morris and John Marshall.

In fact at least ten American presidents had Welsh ancestry, such as Calvin Coolidge, Richard Nixon and Abraham Lincoln, to name just three. The latter's maternal grandparents were called Morris and came from Ysbyty Ifan, North Wales. Five of the first six presidents were of Welsh decent.

+ Thomas Jefferson, author of the Declaration of Independence, supposedly maintained that his father came from Snowdonia.
+ John Marshall was fourth Chief Justice of the United States.
+ Robert Morris became Superintendent of Finance, managing the economy of the United States. He also spent several years in a debtor's prison.

+ Gouverneur Morris (1752–1816) wrote the final draft of the Constitution of the United States. He had one leg, losing the other when he jumped from a window to escape a jealous husband. He died when he pushed a piece of whalebone into his urinary tract to relieve a blockage.

+ President John Adams (1735–1826) the first occupant of the White House, his son President John Quincey Adams and his cousin Samuel Adams (1722–1803), the instigator of the Boston Tea Party in 1773, all descended from the Adams family from Penybanc farm at Llanboidy in Carmarthenshire.

+ Let us consider the name John Evans. It has never been an uncommon name in Wales. So let's pay homage to this ordinary Welsh name by seeing what sort of impact three of the very many John Evanses had across the Atlantic during the eighteenth century.

Now, the first John Evans was a Welsh pirate who died in 1723; he had a short but successful career in the West Indies. He started off in a rowing boat in Jamaica but soon worked his way up to bigger things. On his final voyage across the Caribbean he argued with his bosun, who challenged him to a duel when they reached land. However, on arrival at Grand Cayman, the bosun refused to fight. Captain Evans beat him mercilessly with a cane, which provoked the bosun, who drew his pistol. He shot Evans through the head, killing him instantly.

+ The next John Evans was a politician and even more of a rogue than a pirate. He was born in Wales in 1678 and became colonial governor of Pennsylvania between 1704 and 1709. He was frustrated by the peaceful inclinations of the resident Quakers, who were very influential. He felt that he needed troops to protect the state, so he arranged for a messenger to ride into the Philadelphia fair, shouting that the French were on their way, Evans then rode through the streets with his sword drawn, calling the people to arms. There was panic. People threw their valuables into wells and fled to the forest. It was a complete fabrication and Evans was recalled and retired to Denbigh.

+ Our other John Evans was a weaver who became an explorer. He was born in Waunfawr in Gwynned in 1770 and was sent to make contact with the Mandan tribe of Indians in Missouri, who were believed to speak Welsh. They were thought to be the descendants of Prince Madog's settlement. Evans spent the winter with them but found no trace of Welsh anywhere. He did, however, map the Missouri River, travelling 1,800 miles in sixty-eight days.

Black David the Doctor

David Samwell was born in Nantglyn in Denbighshire in 1751 into a wealthy and educated family, and he became a naval surgeon's assistant. He sailed on Captain Cook's final voyage around the world on HMS *Resolution* between 1776 and 1779, searching for a north-west passage, on this occasion starting from the Pacific. William Bligh was also on board, by the way. When the surgeon Anderson died of consumption, Samwell was promoted to surgeon on the companion ship HMS *Discovery*.

His job was to make sure that the crew remained healthy. Cook had done most of the work himself, since he was committed to keeping his men fit and healthy by keeping scurvy at bay with a diet rich in oranges, lemons and sauerkraut.

Samwell was a respected poet who was noted for a long poem called 'The Padoucan Hunt' about Madog's discovery of America. However, on the voyage he preferred to entertain the sailors with rhymes and bawdy verses. He was a man of appetites who apparently 'revelled in the nymphs of the South Seas, laying any personable female he could'. (Mary McCririck, *Stories of Wales, Book 3*, 1963)

As a poet Samwell took the bardic name Dafydd Ddu Feddyg – Black David the Doctor – which is not a name you will see often in a modern general practice. He was described as 'tall, stout, blackhaired and pock-marked' and possessed of a quick temper. Significantly he kept a journal, and in it he described the death of Cook. Samwell's is the definitive account of his stabbing on the Sandwich Islands (Hawaii) by islanders who appear originally to have believed that he was a god. Samwell's own interests were less spiritual.

- ✦ Richard Wilson from Penegroes (1714–1782), regarded by many as the father-figure of English landscape painting, once exchanged one of his works for a tankard of beer and the remains of a stilton cheese.

- ✦ In 1789 David Watkins, a Quaker from Aberaman, was buried standing up in St John's church in Aberdare so that he could respond quickly to the sound of the Last Trumpet, calling mankind to Judgement.

- ✦ In 1793 Sir William Hamilton invited Quaker whalers from Nantucket to live in Milford Haven. The intention was to develop a whaling fleet to provide the oil needed to support the development of street lighting across the United Kingdom.

- ✦ William Parry (1742–1791) was a well-known portrait painter. One of his works – the *Blind Harpist of Ruabon* – was of his father, John Parry, who was also known as 'a most adept player at draughts'.

- ✦ John Bird from Cardiff, a diarist, wrote about the River Taff in 1790. 'Prodigious quantities of salmon are continually caught in the river, which are all sent off to Gloster and Bristol. Last week upwards of half a ton was conveyed away.'

- ✦ The badger was an occasional part of the diet in Wales. Dr Campbell wrote in 1774, 'being by nature an inactive and indolent creature is commonly fat, and therefore they make his hind quarters into hams in Wales.' (*The Book of Cardiff*)

- ✦ A popular drink in rural Wales in this period was beer warmed with Indian spices.

He believed in the medicinal properties of opium and his death in 1798 at the age of 47 was attributed to an opium overdose – or alternatively to venereal disease. In fact he did write a medical paper called 'The introduction of Venereal Disease into the Sandwich Islands', in which he said that it wasn't the fault of English sailors, but that the infection had found its way from the French in Tahiti. There are some, however, who regard him as being personally responsible.

1780 Aberdaron

Speaking in Tongues

Dic Aberdaron was eccentric; enigmatic; downright odd. He was an important figure in his own time but he is generally forgotten today, remembered only in a poem by R.S. Thomas.

He was born in Aberdaron at the end of the Lleyn Peninsular in 1780 and achieved notoriety for his unusual facility with languages. His father was a carpenter but Dic's apprenticeship was an abject failure. He showed no practical inclinations at all, perhaps through a lack of co-ordination. Dic developed instead an obsession with learning languages. Today we would say that he was a savant; someone on the autistic spectrum but who displays exceptional ability in one particular area.

He left home to escape beatings from an impatient father and spent the rest of his life in transit, learning different languages. It is said that he taught himself Latin before he was 12 and Greek before he was 20. He had a thick beard, a shapeless hat, often wore an old dragoon's jacket and travelled the country with his books and a succession of stray cats, wandering from country house to parsonage looking for sustenance. He always carried with him a large number of books which he sometimes had to sell to buy food or clothing, but he would always try to buy them back with the money he received from patrons.

He is said to have mastered fifteen languages, though in the depths of North Wales it is unlikely anyone knew anything of some of the languages he claimed to speak. Whenever he cleared his throat it probably sounded like a poem in a forgotten language. The story of his learning and of his ability was such that they would believe anything about him. But he was often difficult and generally quarrelsome. Dic received much more generous and understanding treatment then than he would have received today, when he would have been assessed, judged and treated. But in his own time his oddness brought with it a sense of mystery.

There was in some ways a pointlessness about his learning. It was pure, in the sense that it was learning for its own sake because it benefited no one, least of all Dic. He died as penniless and alone as he had lived and was buried in St Asaph in 1843.

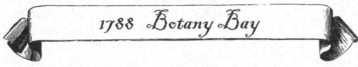

1788 Botany Bay

Building Blocks

The first group of convicts transported to Australia set sail from England in May 1787. It was one of the world's epic voyages. Captain Arthur Phillip led eleven ships sailing in convoy to the other side of the world. They travelled over 15,000 miles in 252 days and no ships were lost. Twenty-two babies were born and sixty-nine persons died en route. When they arrived in January 1788, over 1,400 men and women – convicts, marines and free men – began the European colonisation of Australia. They brought with them supplies to start their lives – like crockery, stoves, tools, seeds, weapons, handcuffs and chains. They even had a prefabricated house for the Governor, including glass for the windows.

And naturally the Welsh wouldn't be left out of such a historic event. There were five identifiably Welsh convicts in the fleet.

There was Mary Watkins from Cowbridge who was about 20 years old when she was sentenced in 1786 to seven years' transportation for stealing clothes to the value of 1s.

William Davis, a baker from Brecon, was transported for life. He died in 1830 after forty-two years in Australia. Shortly after landing he received twenty-five lashes for lighting a fire in his hut.

William Edmunds was originally sentenced to death when he was 29 for stealing a cow in Monmouth in 1785 with a value of 80s. He died in 1843 when he was apparently 87.

Frances Williams was originally sentenced to death on two counts of burglary at Mold but it was commuted to seven years' transportation. She lent her clothes to her friend Elizabeth Pulley when she married Anthony Rope in May 1788. The wedding was celebrated with a fine 'sea pye' containing goat meat, which caused a bit of a problem in the small seaside community, since the goat was stolen. Rope and Pulley went on to have six children. Strange I know, but apparently true.

A man called David Williams, aged 49, was sentenced at Radnor for stealing livestock. The original death sentence was again commuted to seven years' transportation, but he appears to have died before the ships set sail.

The other four, though, helped to build a nation.

+ Captain Cook named part of the eastern coast of Australia New South Wales when he charted it in 1770. Why he did this isn't clear. As we have seen, it was already the name given to the south-west coast of Hudson Bay in Canada by Thomas James in 1631. It is alleged that the name was given because the coastline resembled that of South Wales. I believe that it rains less frequently, however. In 1805 William Bligh (of the HMS *Bounty*) became the fourth Governor of New South Wales.

 1789 Bala

Getting Your Hands Dirty

Betsi Cadwaladr. Wales' very own nursing heroine.

She was born in May 1789 on a farm called Pen Rhiw, above Bala. After running away from home she worked variously as a maid, a housekeeper and a nurse throughout Europe. In 1815 she was in Brussels and tended the wounded lying on the field in the days following the Battle of Waterloo. In 1820 she became nanny to a sea captain's family and spent the greatest part of her life sailing the world.

Late in life, she began nursing in Guy's Hospital and then caring for private patients in their homes. She volunteered for nursing service in the Crimea at the age of 65. She missed the first group that Florence Nightingale took out to the war but in 1854, after a brief period of training, she arrived in Scutari. However, she was a long way from the action and Nightingale refused to let her nurses go to the front. Betsi had come on a mission to care for the wounded and Nightingale seemed to be standing in her way.

Florence described her as 'that wild woman from the Welsh Hills', and threatened to send her home, but instead Betsi headed up to the front to the hospital at Balaclava. What she found there was truly horrific.

'I shall never forget the sights as long as I live,' she said later. The first man she treated had frostbite. 'His toes fell off with the bandages. The hand of another fell off at the wrist.' They were dirty and dying; their wounds had remained untreated for weeks and were infested with maggots. She nursed these men for over six weeks before being put in charge of the kitchen.

On her return in 1855 Betsi, exhausted by over-work and suffering from dysentery, went to live with her sister Bridget in London. She died, forgotten and in poverty, in Shoreditch in the summer of 1860.

Dressing Up

However uncomfortable it might feel, it is absolutely true that modern Druidism has very little to do with the pagan origins that so exercised the Romans that they wanted only to hack Druids up with swords. The Welsh Gorsedd of Bards was founded by Iolo Morganwg in 1792 and they held their first gathering at Primrose Hill in London. It was a cultural organisation which was intended to recognise the Welsh culture, to sing Christian hymns and to allow men to dress up in strange clothes. It probably has very little to do with the pagan heritage, but since no one knows what the originals thought or believed, then Druidism can be made to accommodate just about any idea that you can think of. The image that is presented today is generally a remarkable piece of pantomime based upon misunderstandings and misconceptions.

Iolo Morganwg (1747–1826) was actually Edward Williams, an English-speaking itinerant stonemason and raging drug addict who invented the concept of a Druidic tradition based almost entirely upon documents that he very carefully forged. He invented the Druidic rites of the Eisteddfod. He also invented a bardic alphabet, the 'Coelbren y Beirdd', which contained twenty main letters and twenty mutations.

He organised the first ever Gorsedd of Bards on 21 June 1792 in Primrose Hill in London based, he claimed, on Druidic rites. He had original manuscripts which proved that the Druids had survived the Romans and kept the faith alive. But these documents he had actually written himself, under the influence of laudanum. He took so much of the stuff, it wouldn't be a surprise to learn that he himself actually believed in their authenticity.

It is, however, beyond dispute that whatever the origins of his strange ideas, Williams had a huge effect on Welsh culture and identity. Perhaps it doesn't matter that it was all his own strange invention. It might have been an expression of his own ego but the images of Druids and the oddness of the Eisteddfodau are now part of what binds the Welsh together. Inaccurate perhaps, but full of significance.

1799 Monmouth

Puzzler

John Renie has a unique gravestone; a square of stone upon which a puzzle has been etched, as if it was a large piece of paper on which someone has tried to amuse themselves for an hour or two. It looks like something a boy would do at the back of a particularly boring maths lesson.

What it says is nothing more than 'Here lies John Renie'. A simple sentence, but it can be read, apparently, in 45,760 different ways. Find the H in the middle of the stone and then head in any direction you want and it will spell out the same thing. 'Here lies John Renie'. Up, down, across, round corners … there are 285 individual letters carved into the stone. 15 down, 19 across.

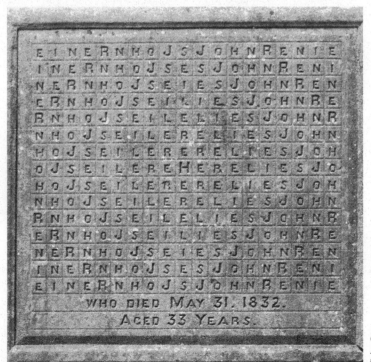

Robert Cutts

+ In 1801 the population of Cardiff was 1,871, making it considerably smaller than either Merthyr or Swansea. By 1871 the population was 57,363.

+ In 1802 Sir William Paxton stood for election as Member of Parliament for Carmarthenshire. He spent the remarkable sum of £15,000 during his campaign. He paid for 11,070 breakfasts, 36,901 dinners, 684 suppers, 25,275 gallons of beer, over 11,000 bottles of whisky and almost 9,000 bottles of cider. He also spent £786 on promotional electoral ribbons. He lost the election by 117 votes.

+ Members of the Lewis-Clark expedition, which established an overland route across America to the Pacific in 1804, met light-skinned Indians in Montana – the Mandans. They had a gurgling kind of language spoken largely through the throat. The explorers believed that they were a long-lost Welsh tribe. Mandan women were highly regarded for their good looks. Apparently they chattered endlessly even when making love, regarded as convincing proof of their Welsh descent. I shall make no comment at all.

+ Sadly, the Mandan tribe was virtually wiped out by smallpox in 1838.

+ There is a memorial in St Mary's church in Tenby to Peggy Davies, who worked as a ladies' bathing attendant for forty-two years. In September 1809, whilst in the sea she 'was seized with apoplexy and expired aged 82.' (*The Cambrian*)

+ John Henry Martin is buried in Ludchurch in Pembrokeshire. At the time of his death in 1823, he was believed to be the last surviving officer who accompanied Captain Cook on his third voyage round the world.

+ In August 1838 two children, one aged 9 and the other 2, were bitten by a rabid dog. They were immersed in the River Usk beneath a bridge; an apparently infallible cure for hydrophobia.

John Renie carved the gravestone himself, in an attempt to confuse the Devil. By the time he had worked out what it said, Renie would have made it to the sanctuary of Heaven. If this is the case, then we sinners have little to worry about. He might be Lucifer, the fallen angel, but apparently he can't do a wordsearch.

Either way, it is lasting memorial at the back of St Mary's in Monmouth to an interesting and talented man. He was born in 1799 and became a house painter and glazier, taking over the family business, they say, at the age of 13 or 14 from their home in Monnow Street. He developed clearly expressed social principles and became a founding member of the Oddfellows, one of the many friendly societies that began in the early nineteenth century.

He died young, aged 33. Perhaps Renie was poisoned slowly by toxic materials, by the lead in the paints and by the arsenic in the wallpapers – painter's colic, as it was called.

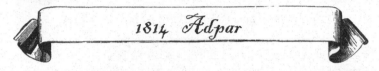

1814 *Adpar*

Alas, Poor Heslop

It was Saturday, 10 September 1814 in Llandyfyriog near Adpar. Thomas Heslop and John Beynon stood on either side of the stream, facing away from each other. They were to walk ten paces before turning and firing. They began to pace out their deliberate steps but after only five paces Beynon turned and shot Heslop in the back. He died almost immediately.

John Beynon was a local solicitor, while Heslop was visiting with some of his friends on a shooting party. It hadn't been a successful visit, but they all gathered together at Beynon's invitation for dinner on Thursday, 8 September 1814 at the Old Salutation Inn in Adpar.

Sadly a dispute developed. Heslop was not happy because he claimed that he hadn't been permitted to shoot when and where he pleased. There had been too many restrictions and this had prevented him from having a good time. He put the blame fairly and squarely on Beynon. As host, Beynon tried to take the heat out of the situation by changing the subject. He started to make derogatory remarks about the barmaid, questioning her virtue and suggesting her availability.

Heslop made strong objections to what Beynon said and, in defence of the poor barmaid, called Beynon a villain and a scoundrel and challenged him to a duel. Beynon accepted. And then, as we have seen, he shot Heslop in the back.

At his trial in Cardigan, Beynon was found guilty of manslaughter, and escaped a lengthy prison term. He was to remain in prison only until his fine was paid, and that was only 1*s*. Public opinion was outraged at this perceived injustice. It is said that he had to go into hiding in a cellar near the bridge in Newcastle Emlyn to escape summary justice. He fled to America, so they say.

Heslop remained in Newcastle Emlyn, the last man to be killed in a duel in Wales. As his grave would have it, 'Alas Poor Heslop'.

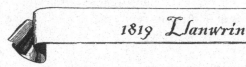

1819 Llanwrin

Sit Down. There is Something I Have to Tell You.

Life in the nineteenth century could be desperate at times, as this story from December 1819 illustrates. Evan Evans, a farmer from Llanwrin, north-east of Machynlleth, was seriously annoyed and took out a prosecution against Hugh Williams, an attorney's clerk. He accused him of 'ravishing' his wife Anne, and transmitting to her a venereal disease. Evans went on to charge Anne with 'whoring'. Marital relations, not surprisingly, were in crisis. And why had it happened? How had she become involved with Hugh Williams?

Anne Evans apparently 'wanted money from him for having connection with her that she might get meat into the house'. The case was dismissed.

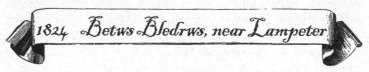

1824 Betws Bledrws, near Lampeter

Tower of Power

The Derry Ormond Tower is a very strange thing. It stands on a hill dominating the views around Betws Bledrws near Lampeter, a genuine nineteenth-century folly.

Much about it appears strangely unclear, for such a big thing. The year of construction isn't certain and neither is its intention.

It is believed to have been built in about 1824 (though some would say 1837) by John Jones, whose family owned the Derry Ormond estate. Once a large estate of over 15,000 acres, it faded away until the mansion was finally demolished in 1952.

The local children were told that it was built so that Jones could see London from the top, to keep an eye on his wife whilst she was shopping. Or to watch for the safe return of ships in the Bristol Channel. The different explanation handed down to adults – though in some ways no less bizarre – is that it was merely a way of providing work for the local unemployed. Men paid to carry out an entirely pointless task? Perhaps it was in fact a model for subsequent developments in the telephone sales industry, but I digress.

Certainly no one ever thought to write anything down about the construction of such a distinctive landmark. It was probably designed by an architect called Cockerell, who also designed St David's College in Lampeter. The builder who directed operations was David Morgan of Llandewi Brefi – we know this because it is so proudly proclaimed on his gravestone.

The tower looks like the upturned barrel of a cannon – allegedly a 'Long Tom', as used at the Battle of Waterloo. It is just under 40m tall, with 365 steps leading up inside to the top. There was even said to be a small wood beneath the tower – crescent shaped – to represent the deployment of Wellington's forces on the battlefield.

Old now, in what is possibly terminal irreversible decay, the tower represents another time. It is the squire doing his bit for the local poor, letting them construct a symbol of his own status. But it has been poorly maintained and has now lost what little importance it once had.

I suggest you keep away. Bits might fall on you.

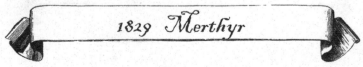

1829 Merthyr

The Red Flag

It would seem that the Welsh have made a habit of designing iconic flags. Just look what Bartholomew Roberts did with a pile of bones. Over a hundred years later they went for an even simpler design, but one which has arguably had an even greater resonance through history.

Things were not happy in Merthyr during the 1820s. The conditions in which people lived and worked were truly awful. People had been drawn there by the availability of work, but living conditions were squalid. Disease was rife. Sanitary arrangements were often non-existent.

When the market for iron slumped in 1829, it was the workers who bore the brunt: dismissal, redundancy, wage reductions, short-term working. Add to this rising prices and you can have some idea of how hard the recession hit those who were already living hand to mouth. Workers worked, suffered and died. There had to be more to life than that.

On 30 May 1829 there was a public meeting in Hirwaun, initially to debate Parliamentary reform, but there were more immediate concerns. A particular grievance was the Court of Requests, which dealt with the recovery of small debts, and the behaviour of the bailiffs, who were repossessing what little property people had. Matters came to a head when bailiffs arrived at the home of Lewis Lewis, with the intention of seizing a cart. Although the bailiffs took possession of a small trunk, a mob marched on Hirwaun, where they reclaimed it from a shopkeeper.

A calf was killed and a white cloth was dipped in its blood. This was raised as a flag to symbolise popular rebellion. A loaf of bread was impaled on a pole to represent the needs of the workers. They marched on Merthyr, ransacking houses and liberating previously recovered property. Shops were attacked and destroyed. The Merthyr Rising, the greatest uprising in Wales since the days of Owain Glyndŵr, had begun.

 1835 Llandovery

The Coachman's Cautionary

On the A40, halfway between Llandovery and Brecon, there is a memorial to a stagecoach disaster – an obelisk enclosed by iron railings, next to a busy road. At the bottom of a steep slope on the other side of the road, the Afon Gwydderig rushes and roars just as it did in 1835. On some maps it is marked simply by the word 'memorial'. But that single word does not do justice to the surprising nature of this simple pillar that stands under the trees in a dark lay-by.

It is one of the earliest warnings against drink-driving – the 'Coachman's Cautionary'.

It marks the spot where the Gloucester to Carmarthen coach plunged off the road and down a precipice on 19 December 1835. According to the inscription, the driver, Edward Jenkins, 'was intoxicated at the time and drove the mailcoach on the wrong side of the road … at full speed (or gallop). The coach went over the 121ft precipice, where at the bottom, near the river, it came against an ash tree, where it was dashed into several pieces'. Colonel Gwynn of Glan Brian Park, Daniel Jones and a man called Edwards were sitting outside, up there with the driver. One of the three inside passengers was a solicitor from Llandovery called David Lloyd Harris.

The memorial was erected as a warning to mailcoach drivers to keep from intoxication. It was designed by J. Bull, Inspector of Mail Coaches, who used the £13 16s 6d he received from forty-one subscribers to erect the obelisk in 1841.

I think it was money well spent. It might not have been as hard-hitting or as effective as recent road safety campaigns, but it has survived a great deal longer.

1839 Llangrannog

The Navigator Lady

Sarah Jane Rees was born in 1839 into a confined life on a small farm in Llangrannog, West Wales. Her father navigated a small boat up and down the coast as a small-time trader. The family wanted her to become a dressmaker, but her ambitions were far more exciting. She went to colleges for ladies in Liverpool and Chester and then finally to a nautical school in London. She qualified as a sea captain and was awarded a master's certificate.

All her life was devoted to others. She taught basic literacy and numeracy skills to farm boys, and advanced navigation to sea captains who came to her school after the children had gone home.

She became very exercised by the role that alcohol played in these remote and isolated communities. Many Welsh women campaigned against alcohol, blaming it for all moral and social ills. Money for food was allegedly spent in pubs. There were always grim days out in the west when the weather closed in and there was only the drink.

In these tiny little communities linked only by the sea, domestic violence was not unusual. Temperance became very much a feminist issue. She believed that women deserved better. The excessive consumption was intimately wedded to domestic violence, the abuse of women and the neglect of children.

Sarah Jane's promotion of women's rights led her to establish a magazine to promote women writers. *Y Frythones* ('The Female Briton') enabled women to participate in public events through the articles that they submitted. In 1865 she was the first woman to be awarded the chair of the Royal National Eisteddfod in Aberystwyth for her poem, 'Y Fodrwy Briodasol'. In 1873 she won the chair in Aberaeron. She adopted the Eisteddfod tradition of a bardic name, one which paid homage to the village that made her – Cranogwen.

Sarah Jane Rees, teacher, poet, editor and temperance campaigner, died in 1916 and is buried in Llangrannog.

✦ In Aberdare in 1841, live fish were seen falling from the sky. In February 1859 in Mountain Ash, small fish fell to earth during a sudden downpour. The fish were still alive and local timber workers filled their buckets with them.

✦ In 1844 Ann Mears went into a Cardiff shop and stole twelve silk handkerchiefs. She held them in her armpit, but when she stretched out her arm to open the door they fell out. She was sentenced to four months' imprisonment, on the basis of her previous good character.

 1852 *Newport*

Bringing the House Down

By July 1852 there was a large Mormon community in Newport and the surrounding villages. To celebrate their faith, they planned a conference to which, according to the *Cardiff and Merthyr Guardian*, elders 'from the camp on the borders of the Great Salt Lake' had been invited, including Dan Jones, a convert who had returned to his native Wales as a missionary. It would be a great occasion, a chance to honour the pioneers who had established a community by the lake after the migration to Utah in 1847. It would also be a chance to celebrate the mission of Dan Jones, who had already baptised about 2,000 converts and translated the Book of Mormon into Welsh. A big reception was planned, miracles anticipated. There might be visions.

At the end of the service the congregation gathered for a tea festival in Sunderland Hall. There were about 400 people present. Inspired. Uplifted. And then there was a creaking noise and one half of the ceiling fell onto the people below.

The noise was such that local residents rushed to the scene to help. They saw some of the congregation dragging themselves from the wreckage, whilst others stayed huddled together beneath tables.

But there was nothing to worry about. Divine agents had chosen to communicate with Newport via dodgy builders and had taken care to ensure that not one person received any injuries in spite of the severity of the incident. The ceiling was heavy – it brought beams down with it – but all survived unharmed. It was noted that the section below which the elders and honoured guests were sitting remained intact.

Clearly this was the miracle they had been hoping for. They spent the rest of the evening giving thanks for their survival. True believers had been saved. They were truly The Chosen Ones. And it would prove such an aid to recruitment too.

The Cambrian newspaper commented wryly, 'this portion of the service however was carried on in another hall, where there was not any risk of another miracle being worked'.

1856 Neath

Alien Abduction – With Free Return

In 1856 Ronald Rhys in the Vale of Neath disappeared for a week after seeing a strange light that was making a loud noise whilst he was going home from work. He went to investigate the light, which was in a field, and suddenly believed he was floating in the air. He then remembered being physically examined by small creatures who helped themselves to a sample of his blood. Then it all went blank. He had no idea he'd been missing for a week until neighbours asked where he had been.

This close encounter left him in quite a state. His skin was covered in scars and had turned bright pink and his hair was falling out. So what was this? Was it a terrible combination of alien abduction and radiation poisoning? Or just Neath beer?

 1857 Aberystwyth

Incident in the Rigging

James Williams was an ordinary boy from Aberystwyth who died at the age of 21. He was serving in the Merchant Navy on the schooner *John and Edward* on 24 May 1857. The schooner took shelter in the harbour of Sarzeau on the north-east coast of Belle Isle, off the coast of Brittany. They had been driven in by the weather and thus the necessary signals were not ready to be hoisted. They anchored close to the stern of a French man-of-war, the *Maratch*. A shot was fired to persuade the British ship to fly its flag. As the sailors worked to do so a second shot was fired and then a third. It was the third shot that hit James as he worked to haul up the colours.

James was in the rigging trying to unfurl the flag but had become entangled in it. The French became impatient and fired a warning shot. It was too well directed. The shot went straight through the flag and James Williams. He died instantly.

In Parliament, Lord Palmerston confirmed that the first two shots were blank musket rounds. The British vessel was at fault, for 'no ship ought to enter the harbour of a foreign country without colours to distinguish her nationality', but there was no justification in ordering a live round to be fired at the ship.

The French offered a full apology to the British Ambassador of 'the most satisfactory and handsome kind'. Orders had already been given to 'dismiss from the French service the officer who had given orders to fire the fatal musket shot'. Palmerston was impressed by the way the whole incident had been handled, saying, 'nothing can be more honourable and proper than the manner of their proceeding towards the English Government on the subject.' (*Hansard*)

Cold comfort to a bereaved family: James' body was brought back home on a French ship on 1 August 1857.

1858 Brecon

Dead in a Toilet

Charles Lumley born in Kent around 1824, became a lieutenant in the army, in the Earl of Ulster's Regiment, and in 1854 he was posted to the Crimea.

It was an awful place; a genuine forerunner for the trench stalemate of the First World War. Just as muddy and just as deadly.

The key strategic feature in the war was Sebastopol. The British planned an attack on a defensive feature called the Redan, to start at dawn on 8 September 1855. The Russian fire was very heavy, but they still managed to fight their way into the Redan. One of the first officers inside was Charles Lumley. As he reached the parapet he attacked three Russian gunners. One of them threw a handful of small cannon shot, which knocked him down. When Lumley got to his feet and urged his men forward, he was shot in the mouth.

It was a severe wound, although not fatal, and he was taken back to the British lines for treatment. The Russians held the Redan.

Lumley was sent home on 29 September 1855 and decorated at the first Victoria Cross investiture in Hyde Park in London on 26 June 1857. He was a hero. But he was a changed man.

He was transferred to Brecon but he found the administrative work difficult. He was eccentric and hot-tempered. Matters came to a head on Sunday, 17 October 1858. The previous day he called his adjutant Richard Davies to his room on a number of occasions, but each time, there was nothing that he wanted. When Davies brought him tea he refused it and walked round and round the barrack square instead. On Sunday morning the household went off to church, but Charles was not there when they returned. His pistol was missing. Davies looked for him.

He didn't have to go far.

He was in the toilet, lying on his left side and he had shot himself behind the right ear.

Charles Lumley VC. Wounded at Sebastopol. Died in a toilet. Buried in Brecon Cathedral.

1856 Swansea

The Needle and the Damage Done

This story is taken from *The Cambrian* newspaper in 1856 and deals with 'an extraordinary operation necessitated by a most singular accident'.

It involved a young Irishman who was, as they say, larking about with some young country women, somewhere in Swansea. He grabbed a 'buxom girl who was engaged in seamstress work' and hugged her.

Big mistake.

When he pressed her to his bosom it turned into an almost fatal embrace. There was a needle in 'the breast of her gown' which penetrated his heart and then broke off. Well, it happens. He was immediately taken to the infirmary where it was decided that the remains of the needle must be extracted since otherwise, 'death must quickly ensue from inflammation of the heart'.

So Dr Green cut through the flesh and 'laid bare the surface of the heart'. He could see the end of the needle and so he pulled it out gently with his forceps. Clearly a triumph, and such delicate skill mightily impressed the newspaper. No surprise there then.

Almost as an afterthought, we are told that since inflammation had already begun, 'it is very doubtful whether his life will be saved'. Regrettable perhaps, but apparently less important than acknowledging

Dr Green's undoubted skills. Perhaps more importantly it was, we are told, to be viewed as a cautionary tale. 'It ought to teach young men before they hug their sweethearts to see that the latter have no needles in their bosoms … The lethal character of Cupid's darts is a mere figure compared with the puncture of such a tiny weapon.'

Wise words indeed.

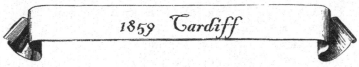

1859 Cardiff

Party Bag

As reported in *The Spectator* magazine in June 1869, a husband in Cardiff encouraged his wife to attend a meeting at the Mormon church. He promised her that she would see 'the angels of the Lord'. During the service the lights were turned out, and she saw figures in white shuffling about. Close by her feet there were strange small figures, rustling as they moved slowly around. The report continues, 'she was probably expected to faint but she seized one of the figures at her feet instead, and put it in her pocket. When she got home she found that it consisted of a few frogs in a white paper bag.'

1865 Patagonia

To the Chubut with a Wheelbarrow

The first 153 Welsh settlers arrived in Patagonia on the *Mimosa* in 1865. It had cost £2,500 to hire the ship for the voyage and make it suitable for passengers. The fare from Liverpool to Patagonia was £12 for adults and £6 for children. There were fifty-six married adults, thirty-three single men, twelve single women and fifty-two children. They had been told that the area was like lowland Wales; they arrived in an arid semi-desert with little food. They trekked across the desert with a single wheelbarrow to carry their belongings. Some died and a baby was born on the march, called Mary Humphries.

When they reached the Chubut River, they built a small fortress at what was to become Rawson, the capital of Chubut. They first made contact with the local Tehuelche people almost a year after their arrival, and they helped the settlement survive the early food shortages.

One of the settlers, Rachel Jenkins, created Argentina's first irrigation system on the Chubut River (or Afon Camwy), irrigating an area 3 or 4 miles to each side of a 50-mile stretch of river. It revolutionised agriculture and created Argentina's most fertile wheatlands.

By 1885 wheat production had reached 6,000 tons, with wheat produced by the colony winning the gold medal at international expositions at Paris and Chicago.

The Lower Chubut valley, inhospitable and desolate when they arrived, was transformed by the Welsh into one of the most fertile, productive agricultural areas in Argentina. They soon expanded the territory into the foothills of the Andes to create a settlement known as Cwm Hyfryd.

By 1915, fifty years after the original settlers arrived, the population of Chubut had grown to 23,000, with about half of these being foreign immigrants. The government wanted to encourage economic growth in Chubut and encouraged European immigrants from southern Europe, as well as a significant number of Argentine nationals and small numbers of Chileans, to settle there and continue the transformational work that the Welsh with a wheelbarrow had begun.

✦ Before the Welsh-speaking colony in Patagonia was established, other locations were considered, including Vancouver in Canada, Australia, New Zealand and Palestine.

 1869 *Yuzovka*

Making Cranes to Build the Ukraine

It seemed quite a sensible thing to do at the time. In 1869 over 100 iron workers from the Welsh Valleys suddenly found themselves in the Ukraine, where they resettled in order to establish the heavy industry required to support the ambitions of the Imperial Russian navy.

It was all because of John Hughes, a Welsh industrialist. He had won the contract from the Czar to provide armour for the ships at the naval base at Kronstadt. Hughes established his facility in 1869 at Alexandrovka near the Sea of Azov and a township grew around the works, called Yuzovka – the Russian for Hughesovka, obviously.

He had been born in Merthyr in 1815, where he had worked as an engineer in the Cyfarthfa Ironworks. His career blossomed and he eventually became a director of the Millwall Engineering and Shipbuilding Company in London, which made a fortune out of covering ships with a wooden frame topped with iron plating. Apparently John Hughes was unable to write and could only read capital letters.

Hughes' success, despite his shortcomings, had attracted the interest of the Russians. So Hughes created the New Russia Company Ltd and sailed to the Ukraine with eight ships full of equipment and specialist ironworkers. A factory was created – along with a town. Soon it had hospitals, schools, churches and a fire brigade. There was even an Anglican church dedicated to St George and St David. By 1900 there was a population of about 50,000.

John Hughes planned it all. Russian workers moved in to learn from the Welsh migrants how to make the ironworks sustainable. Hughes died in 1889 during a business trip to St Petersburg, but the complex continued to expand. Yuzovka became a vital industrial centre and by the end of the nineteenth century it produced 74 per cent of all Russian iron. There was a thriving expatriate community and whilst the Hughes family connection ended with the Russian Revolution in 1917, some Welsh workers remained and their descendants still live there today.

Now Yuzovska is called Donetsk and has a population of over 900,000 and in honour of its origins it is twinned with … Sheffield.

Strange but true.

 1890 *Amlwch*

Forming a Q

It is not perhaps so strange if you are Welsh, but for others it is: two Welsh seamen, both called William Williams and both awarded the Victoria Cross during the First World War. William Charles Williams was killed at Gallipoli in April 1915. But we need to consider the other William Williams, born at Amlwch in Anglesey in 1890.

At the start of the war Williams had enlisted in the Royal Naval Reserve as a seaman and by 1917 he was serving as a gunner on the Q5, a decoy vessel that posed as a merchant ship which, once damaged, would lure German submarines to the surface so that

they could be attacked by secret guns. It was an alarming and dangerous posting. These ships (known as Q-ships) would allow themselves to be struck by a torpedo, sometimes even slowing down to make sure that it happened. In February 1917 the Q5 was indeed hit, flooding the engine room and injuring crew members. The ship sank lower and lower, whilst the gunners remained at their posts behind screens. A 'panic party' even abandoned ship to add to the authenticity. It worked. Submarine U83 surfaced, was attacked and sunk. A triumph. The captain received a VC and Williams a DSM. The damaged Q5 was sold off and a new one commissioned – HMS *Pargust*. The crew resumed their deception in the Atlantic.

Of course, they were attacked again in June 1917. This time a 30ft hole was ripped in the hull, causing significant damage, particularly to one of the screens that shielded the guns from view. Williams took the full weight of the shield on his back to prevent it from falling. Meanwhile the panic party abandoned ship. But the Germans were nervy – and very cautious. They knew about the Q-ships and knew they needed to be absolutely certain. So they didn't surface for at least 30 minutes – with Williams supporting the screen all the time. After it surfaced they continued to wait until the submarine was in the right position. Patience is a virtue – and the U29 was sunk. Williams received his VC in July 1917.

The damage to his back gave him problems for the rest of his life. Despite this he went back to sea again on another Q-ship, the *Dunraven* in the Bay of Biscay. And again they were attacked. This time, however, the submarine refused to be enticed and engaged from a distance, sinking the Q-ship. For this action Williams received a bar to his DSM and was medically discharged in 1918. It is a remarkable service record. William Williams died in 1965 aged 75 and is buried in Amlwch.

1892 Hawarden

Prime Time

William Gladstone, prime minister on no less than four occasions, had, when he was living in what technically was his wife's property, a couple of issues with his eyes.

You see, his chosen form of relaxation was chopping down trees. After a week of amending sub-clauses to parliamentary bills, he liked nothing better than going home to Hawarden to chop down a couple of elms. In fact that is what he was doing when he was first called upon to be prime minister. He paused, rested his axe for a moment and then said, 'my mission is to pacify Ireland', before resuming his labour. To be fair to the man, he always planted a few saplings as a gesture towards long-term sustainability, but he was never as happy as when hacking away at a trunk. On one occasion, however, a splinter flew from the tree and almost blinded him. Then, in 1892, whilst travelling to Chester, a disgruntled voter threw a ginger biscuit through the window of his carriage and almost blinded him in the other eye. Rescuing fallen women was generally much safer.

1894 Aberaman

On Your Bike

It is undoubtedly strange but nonetheless true that the mining village of Aberaman, between Aberdare and Mountain Ash, produced four world-class cyclists at the end of the nineteenth century. The most famous? Arthur Linton, regarded by some as the first sporting victim of performance-enhancing drugs, administered by his trainer Choppy Warburton.

Arthur Linton had started racing in the Cynon Valley. In 1894 he broke four world records and defeated the French champion Jules Dubois in Paris. He was declared Champion Cyclist of the World. However, it was in a road race in 1896 that Arthur Linton had his finest – and last – victory.

He was racing in the Bordeaux to Paris cycle race. It was the longest in the professional calendar at 560km. Arthur was not only the rider but the mechanic too, carrying with him tools and spare tyres. There was some unconventional back-up, though.

In Arthur Linton's obituary in *Cycler's News* the writer, who declares he is one who knew him, states:

> I saw him at Tours, halfway through the race, at midnight, where he came in with glassy eyes and tottering limbs. Choppy and I looked after a wreck – a corpse as Choppy called him, yet he had sufficient energy, heart, pluck, call it what you will, to enable him to gain 18 minutes on the last 45 miles of hilly road.

We can't be sure what Choppy gave him but it was almost certainly something a little stronger than encouragement. To recover 18 minutes of lost time in 45 miles was remarkable. What he gave him was probably heroin. The other drugs of choice were cocaine and strychnine, though none of them were really performance-enhancing. All they did was dull the pain. Whatever it was, it enabled him to set a record time.

Arthur Linton died six weeks later in Aberdare in June 1896, perhaps because of the drugs he was given. He was 28 years old.

 1896 Saundersfoot

I Believe I Can Fly

Forget what you were taught. It wasn't the Wright brothers who first mastered powered flight in America and changed the world. If you live in Pembrokeshire, you will believe that Bill Frost did that seven years earlier, in 1896. Saundersfoot, the birthplace of aviation.

Frost is said to have set off from a field at St Bride's Hill on 24 September 1896 and stayed airborne for 10 seconds.

Bill Frost was a carpenter and builder and he had been working on his project since 1880. His interest had started in 1876 when as a carpenter carrying a plank of wood, he had been lifted off the ground in a high wind. As a result, flying became his obsession. In the 1890s he was often seen running around the countryside with a zinc sheet strapped to his head, though many said he was still grieving the premature deaths of his wife and daughter.

He applied for a patent for his invention in 1894. It was a hybrid, called the Frost Airship Glider, for good reason. It was propelled upwards by two reversible fans. Once in the air, it spread its wings and moved as the wings tilted. His machine was 31ft long, made of bamboo canvas and wire, with hydrogen-filled bags. Whether it actually represented powered flight is another point entirely. Perhaps it was just an elaborate glider.

Frost was adamant that it worked. He said it took off and flew for about 500 yards before the undercarriage caught in a tree and he crashed in a field. If it hadn't been for the tree he would have been away, out to sea, so perhaps it did him a favour. Sadly the event was not witnessed.

Sadly, the flying machine was then battered and destroyed in gales. When Frost went to London to get funding for his invention he was ridiculed by the War Department, who assured him that they had no intention of adopting aerial navigation as a means of warfare.

He died in 1935, a pioneer of the air – but ignored and unregarded.

 1899 Pontardawe

Can You Keep a Secret? Possibly.

That's the problem with being a double agent. No one is ever completely sure which side you are on. Arthur Owen, born in Pontardawe in 1899, was a perfect example. His was a true story and a strange one. He was an electrical engineer who played a crucial part in the Second World War as a Welsh double agent.

Owen had a company that made batteries for ships and he was a civilian contractor for both the Royal Navy and the German navy too. The British Secret Service initially questioned him on what he saw in German shipyards, but then he was recruited by a German intelligence agency in 1938. As a Welsh nationalist he had little loyalty to the British authorities but this approach unsettled him and he reported the contact. Was it true? Was it a double bluff? Could he be trusted?

He was interred in Wandsworth Prison but it was felt he would be more useful as a double agent. He had the code name 'Snow' and established links with the Germans that he reported back.

+ A legendary Victorian circus elephant, Jwmbi, is thought to have been buried in the grounds of a Tregaron hotel after dying on tour in 1848. Jwmbi was part of Batty's Travelling Menagerie. Sadly excavations have been unable to find the remains.

+ The great-grandmother of Harriet Beecher Stowe, author of *Uncle Tom's Cabin*, was born in Llandewi Brefi.

+ In 1872 the philosopher Bertrand Russell was born in Trellech in Gwent.

+ For every person who emigrated to America from Wales in the nineteenth century, there were twenty-five immigrants from Ireland.

+ Police records from 1860 indicate that at that time there were 420 prostitutes working in Butetown.

+ In the league table of drunkenness in Newport in 1886, the top three positions were held by labourers with 136 convictions, followed by seamen with 54 and drunk married women with 49.

+ In 1882 Morris John Jones of Maentwrog, a 33-year-old farmer and butcher, was sentenced to twelve months' hard labour for stealing eighty-seven sheep.

+ Jesse James (1847–1882), the notorious American outlaw, was of Welsh descent. He was a young man with seriously psychotic inclinations.

+ William Jones from Dinas was a soldier in the 7th Cavalry who was killed in the ill-fated Battle of the Little Bighorn with General Custer in 1876.

LC-USZ62-3854

The Germans used him to supply identities and ration books for their agents. He delivered German spies to MI5, who were given the choice of becoming double agents themselves or being shot. Most did not find this a difficult decision and through them vital information was gathered. Ironically the Germans actually employed the agents who helped destroyed them.

But the British were never very sure that they could trust him. If he was on anyone's side, it was his own. His motivation was not patriotic; rather, it was financial. In fact it appears that he told the Germans that he was a double agent – but strangely they did nothing about it. He was interned again, this time in Dartmoor. But even there he continued to work for MI5 by gathering information from German inmates.

At the end of the war he emigrated to Canada to escape possible reprisals from either side. Eventually he moved to Ireland, where he died in 1957. His daughter was the Hollywood actress Patricia Owen, best known for her role as the unfortunate wife in the classic horror film *The Fly*. She never talked about Arthur – perhaps to protect him. Suspicion and distrust runs deep in the world of the double agent.

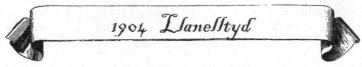

1904 Llanelltyd

Being Certain

Frances Power Cobbe, campaigner and journalist, social reformer and suffragette was buried in North Wales in April 1904, and her will contained an unexpected condition. She instructed that doctors should 'perform on my body the operation of completely and thoroughly severing the arteries of the neck and windpipe'. The strange request to virtually cut off her head was to be carried out to 'render any revival in the grave absolutely impossible'. In this way she could laugh in the face of a great fear of the time – that your death had been misdiagnosed and that you should awake, buried alive. If it wasn't carried out – or indeed witnessed by one of the executors – then all bequests in the will were invalid.

The funeral itself was simple. No mourning dress worn, and 'her coffin [was] plain and simple and made of the most perishable material on the principles of earth to earth burial', as the local newspaper reported.

She had been found dead in bed at Hengwrt, where she had lived with her companion Mary Lloyd, a sculptor to whom she regarded herself as married. Frances was 81 years old and was buried alongside Mary, who had died in 1896.

Frances devoted her life to radical views, campaigning at different times for improvements in reformatory schools and women's rights and finally settling on animal rights. She opposed cruelty in all its forms and especially 'tortures inflicted by the vivisectors on helpless animals for the purposes of demonstrations and experiments'.

Power Cobbe wrote hundreds of articles, the first called 'The Rights of Man and Claims of Brutes'. Through her relentless campaigning she managed to influence public opinion and she soon became President of the British Union for the Abolition of Vivisection.

Of course, she made herself very unpopular. She was seen as eccentric, dressing 'in a masculine style' and being of 'great bodily size'. Indeed, in an act of revenge she herself was accused by her opponents of cruelty to horses, which led to a lengthy court case – at the end of which the accusation was dismissed.

You will not, I think, be surprised to learn that whilst the operation upon her dead body was successfully performed by Dr Hadwen from Gloucester, the financial arrangements in her will were disputed.

1905 Cardiff

Hen Wlad Fy Nhadau

The words written by Evan James, poet and weaver, and the music composed by his son James in Pontypridd in 1856, have come for many to represent the identity and spirit of Wales. *Hen Wlad Fy Nhadau*, the Welsh national anthem, was originally called *Glan Rhondda* and was first sung by Elizabeth John in the vestry of Tabor Methodist chapel in Maesteg. James James played his harp at local dances and the tune was originally played at a much faster rate than today. It was slowed down to allow it to be sung by large crowds. It wasn't a commissioned piece; it evolved into an anthem as a result of its popularity, which perhaps explains its strength.

The breakthrough came at the Llangollen Eisteddfod in 1858, when it was published in a collection of music called 'Gems of Welsh Melody'. It sold in large numbers, to be sung in chapels and parlours. It became a feature of all subsequent eisteddfodau. Its position was sealed at the National Eisteddfod at the Albert Hall in London in 1887. Prince Albert Edward, the Prince of Wales, turned up. The crowd rose as one and sang 'God Bless the Prince of Wales'. In return, at the end of the proceedings when *Hen Wlad Fy Nhadau* was sung, the Prince of Wales and family unexpectedly got to their feet, thus giving final approval to its status as a national anthem.

The title translates into English as '(Old) Land of my Fathers' though one is always reminded of what Dylan Thomas said: 'Land of my fathers? My fathers can have it.' That hasn't stopped it being adopted by others though. In Cornwall it is called *Bro Goth Agan Tasow* and in Brittany it trips merrily off the tongue as *Bro Gozh ma Zadou*.

In the original Welsh version, it was the first national anthem to be sung at the start of a sporting event. It happened in 1905, when Wales played a rugby international against New Zealand. They, of course, started the match with the Haka. So the Welsh player Teddy Morgan led the crowd in the singing of *Hen Wlad Fy Nhadau*. Wales won 3–0 and its position was assured.

+ In 1909 the National Eisteddfod was held in the Albert Hall in London. Prime Minister H.H. Asquith was guest speaker, and suffragettes saw this as an opportunity to protest. The Archdruid composed a poem, attacking the suffragettes for disrupting the celebration of the bards and called for the women to be imprisoned.

+ Following the tireless work of Welsh missionaries in north-east India in the nineteenth century, by 1901 around 20,000 people in Assam worshipped in Welsh-style chapels.

+ In 1912 Sarah Williams of Manordeilo, described as a woman of 'bad character', claimed that she had been seduced by Fred Ridley, who had entered her cottage by sliding down the chimney.

1909 Chubut

Raindrops … Would Have Put the Fire Out

Lewis Jones was a Welsh colonist who settled in the Chubut Valley of Patagonia. He was murdered by two American vagrants mistakenly identified as Butch Cassidy and the Sundance Kid. Jones ran a general store in Esquel, and in December 1909 resisted a robbery and refused to give up the takings. That night, Butch Cassidy and the Sundance Kid (apparently) set fire to the curtains of his home and he badly burned his hands putting out the fire. The next day they returned to the store and killed him. Jones was unable to defend himself because of his burns.

In fact they are now believed to have been called William Wilson and Robert Evans. Cassidy and Sundance had probably been killed the previous year. Some people do believe, though, that Butch Cassidy killed a Welsh settler in 1903.

+ Charles 'Cowboy' Morgan Evans (1903–1969), who won the World Series Rodeo Bulldogging Championship at Madison Square Gardens in New York in 1927, was of Welsh descent.
+ Frank Lloyd Wright (1867–1959), the great American architect, was proud of his Welsh heritage. He called his Wisconsin home Taliesin. His mother was born in Llandysul.

1910 Monmouth

The Man Who Fell to Earth

Charles Rolls' enthusiasm for cars and excitement gave him a career. When he was a student he had the first car ever in Cambridge. As a result he became known as 'Petrolls'. They are clever in Cambridge, they say.

Rolls opened exclusive car showrooms in Mayfair and after a visit to Manchester in 1904 he agreed to take the whole car output of Royce Limited, which would then be sold exclusively by Rolls under the name of Rolls-Royce.

Charles Rolls' success in various motoring competitions promoted the reputation of their cars. The 1907 Scottish Reliability Trial involved driving 15,000 miles, after which any worn parts were replaced. The Silver Ghost won, with the necessary replacements costing just over £2. As a result, the motoring press described it as 'the best car in the world' and the reputation of Rolls-Royce was sealed.

However, Rolls' great passion was flying. He was the second person to be awarded a pilot's licence by the Aero Club in March 1910. His greatest flight was on 2 June 1910, when he made the first flight from England to France and back again, non-stop across the English Channel. He became a national hero. 'He electrified the entire kingdom by his exploits', claimed the papers.

But six weeks later he was dead. *The Daily Journal* in Knoxville, Tennessee reported the accident:

Daring Aviator Dashed to Death

Hon. Chas. Rolls Instantly Killed at Bournemouth in the presence of Spectators.

It was a flying tournament, the prize going to whomever could land their plane nearest to a given mark in front of the grandstand. Rolls was flying a Wright's biplane, which had been modified without authorisation. The tailpiece snapped off and the framework crumpled. It fell 100ft from the sky and shattered completely on impact. When Charles was eventually dragged from the tangled wreckage, it was found that he had fractured his skull. Such was his fame that speeches were interrupted in the House of Lords to announce his death.

He was the first Briton to die in an air accident.

1911 Llanelli

Under Fire

Llanelli played a crucial part in the first national rail strike in August 1911. Workers were protesting at wages of £1 per week, below the national average for other skilled manual labourers. They were supported by colliers and tinplate workers.

The town had a strategic position, sitting on the Great Western Railway between England and the Troubles in Ireland. Around 500 men blockaded Llanelli's two level crossings; a disruption that could not be tolerated. The strike started on 19 August and after two days the Home Secretary Sir Winston Churchill responded to a request to send in troops from the Royal Worcester Regiment to maintain order. This request had come from local grocer, councillor and magistrate Thomas Jones – who was also a shareholder in the railway company. He was not keen on a dispute interfering with his dividends.

The Worcesters tried to clear a way for a train with a bayonet charge. They made it through one level crossing but the strikers swarmed aboard and raked out the fire. The troops who had followed the train were trapped in a cutting, surrounded by stone-throwing strikers.

Major Stuart ordered the Justice of the Peace to read out the Riot Act and then ordered his men to fire. Two young men, Jac John and Leonard Worsell, who were in their own gardens and not involved at all, were shot. Worsell in fact was from Penge in South London and was being treated for tuberculosis at Allt y Mynydd Sanitorium. He went outside mid-shave to see what was going on and was shot through the heart – accidentally, according to the major. Witnesses, however, said that both men were targeted. One soldier refused to fire on the crowd and deserted.

The shooting resulted in a riot, involving not just the strikers but other residents of Llanelli. Shops and businesses were attacked. The first target was Thomas Jones' shop. The police station was also attacked. Protesters who were injured by bayonets and batons refused to attend hospital, fearing arrest.

Civil disturbance, anger, the threat of a mutiny – these were difficult moments. One man was killed when he used dynamite to break into an armoured freight carriage. It contained munitions which exploded. Three others with him died later from their injuries.

The irony was that whilst all this was going on, the trade dispute was settled by an improved pay offer; calm was restored. Burleigh-Stuart was promoted and ended his career as a brigadier general.

And for many years the Worcestershire cricket team were known locally as 'The Murderers'.

◆ It was indeed a most unlikely friendship. Winston Churchill, who as Home Secretary had sent the troops on to the streets not only in Llanelli but also in Tonypandy to maintain law and order by supporting the police against striking miners in 1910. Winston Churchill, whose condemnation of the miners' strike led to the General Strike of 1926. Winston Churchill, who went out of his way to help his friend, a Welsh miner …

Churchill and John Williams had served together in France during the First World War in the 6th Battalion of the Royal Scots Fusiliers. Williams wrote to him in desperation in 1929, seeking employment, and Churchill used his influence to get him a post in the Ministry of Defence.

 1913 Broadstone, Dorset

Selected, Naturally

It is strange but true that a man from Wales beat Charles Darwin to it. And yet, Alfred Russel Wallace has become a sadly neglected figure, overshadowed by Darwin.

He was born in Llanbadoc in Monmouthshire, and he was apprenticed as a surveyor at his brother's company in Neath. He claimed descent from William Wallace of Scotland, but he had been selected to begin his researches in Neath. To be honest he was never much more than an Englishman who lived in Wales for a while, since his parents were both English and he even referred to himself as such, but it is nice to think that a couple of years in Neath turned his head. It has happened before. And what better place can there be in which to confront the peculiarities of evolution? Certainly his interests grew when he joined different societies in Neath.

In 1845 Wallace went on an expedition to South America to collect specimens from the Amazon Basin. The intention was to collect insects to sell to collectors. Throughout his time there he maintained contact with Neath, sending back specimens that reflected his interest in evolution as often as possible. He spent four years in the Amazon but serious illness forced him to return home. His ship *The Helen* caught fire in the mid-Atlantic and he spent ten days in an open boat before being rescued. Sadly his huge collection of specimens was lost.

Wallace lived in London for a while on the insurance payments he received for the lost collection, before leaving for Indonesia. He caught malaria and this triggered a keen sense of mortality. He formed a theory of natural selection – or 'survival of the fittest'. Wallace outlined his thoughts in a letter to Charles Darwin, who he knew was passionate about the same subject. This sent Darwin into a frenzy, his own work being far from complete. He rushed to finish *On the Origin of Species*.

Perhaps Wallace was not the fittest.

He was a great scientist who revolutionised human thought, but he had no private wealth and struggled financially for the whole of his life. It was Darwin, in fact, who managed to get him a small government pension in 1881. Wallace died in 1913 in Broadstone in Dorset.

1913 Newport

Trapped in Newport

Harry Houdini, the showman and escapologist, made no secret of his plan to throw himself off the transporter bridge in Newport. It had been a key feature of his week on the stage at the Newport Empire. He had previously leapt into San Francisco Bay with his hands handcuffed behind his back and a 75lb iron ball attached to one ankle. The River Usk and Houdini were destined to meet.

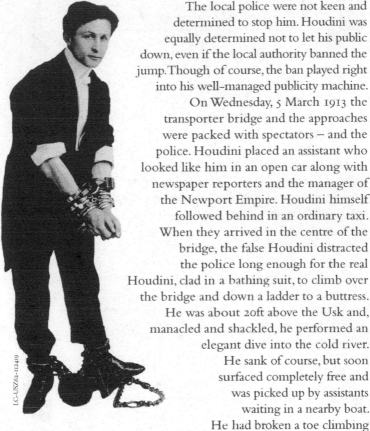

The local police were not keen and determined to stop him. Houdini was equally determined not to let his public down, even if the local authority banned the jump. Though of course, the ban played right into his well-managed publicity machine. On Wednesday, 5 March 1913 the transporter bridge and the approaches were packed with spectators – and the police. Houdini placed an assistant who looked like him in an open car along with newspaper reporters and the manager of the Newport Empire. Houdini himself followed behind in an ordinary taxi. When they arrived in the centre of the bridge, the false Houdini distracted the police long enough for the real Houdini, clad in a bathing suit, to climb over the bridge and down a ladder to a buttress. He was about 20ft above the Usk and, manacled and shackled, he performed an elegant dive into the cold river. He sank of course, but soon surfaced completely free and was picked up by assistants waiting in a nearby boat. He had broken a toe climbing down the ladder, but was otherwise unscathed. A triumph, though of course not a surprise.

But the police wouldn't leave it alone. On the Saturday night Houdini was pleased to announce that he had been given two summonses: one accused him of obstructing the public highway and the other of holding a public entertainment on Newport Bridge. How grateful he must have been for the continuing publicity. The police said he'd given his word of honour that he wouldn't jump, but Houdini denied it. They said they had been concerned that when the crowd rushed to one side of the bridge to watch him, it might have collapsed.

Pretty feeble, and of course the case was dismissed.

Harry Houdini, 'the Master of Manacles', was set free once more.

1914 Pembroke Dock

Training

On their tombstones they are both described as 'Boy'. Robert Handel Mendelsohn Griffiths from Dorchester and James O'Brien from Kensington. Both members of the Border Regiment, they were buried in the Military Cemetery in Pembroke Dock in 1914.

They had both enlisted as 'Boy Soldiers' and had been stationed in Carlisle. In July 1914 the battalion had been sent to Pembroke Dock and had been involved in training exercises at Rosebush. Then on 4 August orders were received for general mobilisation and Robert and James were sent by rail from Carlisle to join their colleagues. What excitement. Grown up at last. Ready to fight for their country. Ready to be heroes. What an adventure.

On 29 August 1914 whilst travelling by train between Tenby and Pembroke Dock to join their battalion, they were both struck on the head by the open door of a railway carriage travelling in the other direction whilst they were leaning together out of the window. Robert died instantly. James died three days later.

They were both 17 years old.

1916 Bucharest

A Street Carmen Named Roumania

Queen Elisabeth of Romania died in Bucharest in 1916. Her daughter's remains were exhumed and reburied close to her mother. You may wonder what this has to do with Wales. It is strange and it is true that she was responsible for the marketing sound bite that Llandudno had been looking for. After a five-week stay she described it as 'a beautiful haven of peace'. Translated into Welsh as 'Hardd, Hafan, Hedd', it became the official motto of the town.

She stayed at the Adelphi on the Promenade, now known as the Marine Hotel. She had asked a Romanian diplomat in London to find her a place for quiet contemplation. After a word with the Prince of Wales, Llandudno is what Prince Gyhka came up with.

To be honest, it might not feature at the top of any list you might offer, but the Prince of Wales laid on his own personal train and she arrived on the North Wales coast in 1890.

Elisabeth had once been considered as a possible consort for the future Edward VII and had (rather oddly) formed unshakable Republican beliefs. The writer James Carleton Young said of her that she would 'renounce her throne, live in a peasant's hut ... if thereby she might bring happiness and prosperity to her people'. She was certainly noted for her charitable works but she was a sad and rather haunted figure. 'She lost heart when her only child the Princess Maria was borne to eternal rest' in 1874 at the age of 3. (James Carleton Young, writing in *The Outlook*, 1 October, 1904)

This made the Romanian royal succession rather complicated; hence the need for a restful time at the seaside. But it wasn't quite as contemplative as she had hoped. She was taken to the National Eisteddfod at Bangor, where she was admitted to the Gorsedd of Bards under her pen name of Carmen Sylva. She was a published poet and novelist in four languages, though none of them Welsh. She was taken on boat trips, she had a command performance from the local Punch and Judy man, yet none of this put her off.

Elisabeth was for a short time the centre of social life in the town and her stay has been remembered in street names like Carmen Sylva Road and Roumania Crescent.

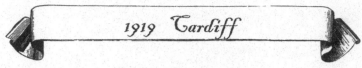

1919 Cardiff

The Cardiff Trouser Riots

Oh yes, they were real enough. Strange as it may seem, four men died in riots in the hot June of 1919. Many more were seriously injured. Houses burned. Knives were carried. Guns fired. Fear stalked the street – and all too soon there were race riots.

The world seemed to be disintegrating. The First World War was followed by the Spanish Influenza outbreak that killed millions. Everything seemed fragile, unfamiliar, threatening. There was a shortage of houses, a shortage of jobs – and the rich ethnic diversity of Cardiff was an easy scapegoat for everything that seemed wrong with the world.

The problems began in Newport on 6 June, when an African man was said to have insulted a local woman. Lodging houses were attacked. Chinese laundries trashed. A rioter, given perhaps more publicity oxygen than he deserved by the press said, 'We went to France and came back to find these foreigners have got our jobs and houses'.

The troubles soon spread to Cardiff. Shots were fired. Fred Longman, a discharged soldier, was stabbed and killed by a West Indian, Charles Emmanuel. Another man, Harold Smart, was killed when his throat was opened by a razor. Houses were ransacked in Bute Street and Adamsdown.

The chief constable, David Williams, made his own measured intervention. He suggested, quite seriously, that black men should be prevented from wearing white flannel trousers when playing cricket. They were 'more revealing than corduroys and make black men more attractive to white girls. Young Cardiff girls should not be allowed to admire such beasts'.

I want some of those trousers. Now.

Notwithstanding such measured analysis, riot and disorder settled upon Cardiff. The Princess Royal Hotel on Millicent Street was set alight for offering rooms to foreigners. A woman married to an African was stripped and her teeth knocked out. Lynch mobs patrolled the streets.

There were riots across the UK; a heady cocktail of racism and economic uncertainty, but nowhere else in the country was the blame laid so confidently upon a pair of trousers.

Some immigrant workers left Cardiff as a result, and a few asked to be repatriated. But many others remained where they were as the disturbances faded away and so ensured that Cardiff became the vibrant and ethnically rich city it is today.

+ Harold Lloyd (1893–1971), the early cinema star, was of Welsh descent. In 1919 he lost a thumb and forefinger when a prop bomb went off during a photo shoot.

+ The actor Richard Burton was born in 1925 in Pontrhydyfendigaid near Port Talbot, where Anthony Hopkins was born in 1937.

+ The comedian Tommy Cooper (1922–1984) was born in Caerphilly. Born premature, he was not expected to survive. It is said that his grandmother kept him alive on a mixture of condensed milk and brandy.

+ The Welsh Pig Society was formed in 1920 in order to protect and promote the Welsh pig breed. By 2000 it was an endangered species.

+ In October 1924 Rose Grey, 45 years old, appeared before Cardiff magistrates for the 130th time. She was charged with behaving in a riotous manner in Bute Street and assaulting Police Constable Arnold Cooper. She was sentenced to three months' imprisonment. As she was taken away she shouted at Cooper, 'May God forgive!'

+ James Henry Richards was a master baker and he had been trading in Rhymney for thirty years without blemish. However, he was prosecuted in 1924 for selling loaves that were underweight. His pound loaves were significantly less than 1lb. His defence was that the bread was especially hard baked, because that is what the customers wanted. Because they were in the oven half an hour longer than normal, they lost weight during the process as the water was driven out. An interesting try perhaps, but he was found guilty and fined 20s.

Breaking the Mould

Merlin Pryce was the Welshman who made a crucial contribution to the discovery of penicillin, possibly the greatest discovery in the history of medicine. It is always ascribed to Alexander Fleming, and yet without Merlin Pryce from Merthyr, it would not have been possible.

He was born in Troed y Rhiw in 1902 and educated in Merthyr, Pontypridd and the Welsh National School of Medicine. He was awarded a Junior Research Scholarship under Fleming in the Bacteriology Department at St Mary's Hospital Medical School.

According to Pryce's sister, the key date in the discovery of penicillin occurred when Fleming came back from his summer holidays in 1928. Pryce went to see him on his first day back in work and he (allegedly) was the one who noticed the mould in the petri dishes. They had been left in the laboratory when they should have been cleared away. It was Pryce who saw that no bacteria surrounded this mould, which might have drifted in through an open window overlooking Praed Street. So if he hadn't noticed it, so the story goes, then penicillin would not have been discovered so soon. Certainly, many still believe that he deserves greater recognition.

He went on to build a distinguished career for himself as a professor of pathology in St Mary's. For his part Pryce always played down his role in the laboratory on that fateful morning, and always made it clear that the credit should lie entirely with Fleming.

+ In June 1928 Amelia Earhart's seaplane landed in the water at Burry Port. She was the first woman ever to fly across the Atlantic. The crossing from Newfoundland took twenty hours. She arrived in the plane *Friendship* – as a passenger. She had the title of Assistant Pilot but the plane was flown by Wilmer Stultz and Lou Gordon. Sadly they have been largely forgotten and the glory of an aquatic landing in the Loughor Estuary remains with Amelia.

But it seems that Merlin Pryce from Merthyr was involved somehow. He died in 1976.

1929 Chicago

The St Valentine's Day Massacre

Llewelyn Morris Humphreys (1899–1965) succeeded Al Capone as Public Enemy No.1 in America in 1931 – and his parents came from Wales. Brian Humphreys and Ann Wigley from Carno near Newtown in Powys emigrated to Chicago to escape poverty. Their son Llewelyn became involved in crime. He changed his name to Murray, since no one could pronounce Llewelyn, and became infamous as Murray the Hump. Soon he was absorbed into Al Capone's mob.

He was a cold-blooded killer when required, but generally he was much more comfortable with money laundering, which he invented. He was dapper and softly spoken, betraying no emotion when ordering a murder or a beating. He was known as The Clever Hood and his talents made him Capone's second in command. He managed bootlegging operations which made huge amounts of money in the time of Prohibition. He is also believed to have organised the St Valentine's Day Massacre on the street where he was brought up in Chicago.

But of course, he was kind to old ladies and gave silver dollars to the needy. He looked after recently released convicts. But he may also have murdered his lover's husband with an ice pick.

He acknowledged his Welsh origins when his daughter was named Llewella in 1934. He was a devoted father, arranging for Frank Sinatra to appear at her birthday parties. He taught her to pretend to shoot anyone who upset her. Llewella was a talented pianist and she was tutored in Europe, where she performed

---

+ Tommy Farr from Clydach Vale, one of the greatest British-born heavyweight boxers, was renowned for his singing voice. He recorded some ballads accompanied by George Formby on the ukulele.

recitals in a number of opera houses. In Rome she began a relationship with the actor Rossana Brazzi, who became the father of her son, Murray's only grandson. However, she suffered from mental illness and in 1958 Murray arranged for her to be admitted to a sanatorium in Kansas.

Despite his criminal career, he spent only a brief period in prison. He died of a heart attack in 1965 and is buried in a blue marble crypt, which is now in the middle of a trailer park in Oklahoma.

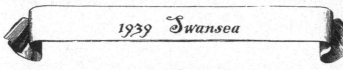

1939 Swansea

Dai the Spy

His name was Gwilym Williams, though perhaps inevitably he came to be known as 'Dai the Spy'. And he is regarded as the best spy the country ever had.

Gwilym had an undistinguished record as a police officer in Swansea, where he had been reprimanded for drinking whilst on duty and apparently assaulting residents. He retired from the force before the outbreak of war – and became the perfect double agent.

MI5 invented the idea of a hardcore cell of Welsh Nationalists, ready to sabotage the English infrastructure, and Hitler promptly offered Home Rule for Wales in an attempt to destabilise the country. Gwilym Williams' cover was established by membership of Plaid Cymru and he was sent to Belgium to infiltrate German military intelligence. The Germans accepted him as a Welsh Nationalist leader, keen to lead sabotage missions, largely because he had memorised the names of prominent members of the Welsh Nationalist Party. It was apparently enough for them.

The message he took them was that the war was an opportunity the Welsh could not afford to miss. He told the Germans that he had arrived in Belgium with the approval of 'WW', the code name for an agent they believed that they had inside Plaid. They didn't know he was a British double agent.

The scene was set for Gwilym to plant false information and to uncover German planning. The only training he received was the advice to say 'I beg your pardon' whenever he was asked a question. This would buy himself some additional thinking time. And on the basis of such valuable advice Gwilym was highly effective: he was able to uncover plans to land a U-boat at Penmaen in Gower, a plot to steal a Spitfire and one to pour poison into Cray reservoir near Brecon. He also uncovered a spy ring working from the Spanish Embassy in London.

It was dangerous work – he risked death if he was caught. But he wasn't. He served his country well, survived and died in 1949, aged 62.

+ The real name of the singer Ricky Valence, who had a No.1 hit with 'Tell Laura I Love Her' in September 1960 was David Spencer from Ynysddu near Newport. He was born in 1939. Later in life he became a born-again Christian.

 1940 *Blaenau Ffestiniog*

What's in Your Quarry?

In 1940 the government was anxious about the safekeeping of the country's greatest art treasures. The original plan to ship them off to Canada was rejected, since U-boats controlled the Atlantic. So a different plan was needed to make art invasion-proof. They arranged for them to be moved from museums and galleries and taken to the Manod Quarry in Blaenau Ffestiniog. It was a disused slate quarry hollowed out of a mountain, chosen because it was isolated and largely bombproof. Soon it was enlarged and adapted. Behind two huge steel doors in the hillside was a 300-yard tunnel leading to huge storage rooms and small brick buildings constructed inside the caves to maintain optimum conditions.

Soon Rembrandts, Turners and Holbeins all rubbed frames with the work of da Vinci as well as the Crown jewels.

They were taken to North Wales in vans disguised as delivery vehicles for a chocolate company. One truck had a particularly difficult journey. It was carrying the extremely large canvas of *King Charles on Horseback* by Van Dyck. In order for it to pass under low bridges, the truck's tyres had to be deflated and then reinflated once it was through. The lorries drove up to the door and the treasures were pushed in wagons along a narrow-gauge railway system. One painting a month was taken back to London to go on public display to reassure the public that they were not lost, and then returned to Manod.

The quarry manager was given the responsibility of looking after them. Friends later said that the responsibility shortened his life. Curators from the National Gallery lived in nearby Pengwern Hall. Two brothers were employed to maintain the ventilation system and they stuck to their task, even after the galleries were emptied. The government had a forty-year lease on the caves which expired in 1981, but they refused to relinquish their tenancy. The fearful thought that they might be required again could never be entirely erased.

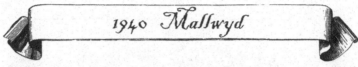

1940 *Mallwyd*

And are there still Damson Jam Sandwiches for Tea?

At the beginning of September 1940 the Germans bombed Liverpool. They were naturally keen to find out how well they had done. Hitting your targets was just as important then as it is today in our modern corporate world.

So they sent out reconnaissance missions to check on what they had achieved and a Junkers Ju 88 was dispatched from an airfield near Paris to find out. The commander was Hans Kauter, a photo intelligence officer who had attended Cambridge University.

They were spotted by Spitfires from RAF Hawarden and the Junkers was attacked over North Wales. The port engine was disabled by cannon fire, but it managed to disappear into cloud and the Spitfires, running out of fuel, had to return to base. But the Junkers was unable to climb over the Welsh hills and it made a forced landing near Mallwyd at the southern end of Snowdonia. There was no fire and the aircraft was largely intact but the crew were all injured. Kauter, with cuts and bruises and broken ribs, was the most mobile. So he destroyed documents, disposed of his revolver and went off in search of help.

He followed the Afan Clywedog for about 2 miles until he reached the farmhouse of Gelli Ddolen. Jane Jones, the farmer's wife, was busy making damson jam but took time out to let him in. Naturally she gave him a cup of tea and a jam sandwich – it would have been rude not to – and then left Hans in the kitchen whilst she went to tell her husband Idwal, at work in the fields, about their unexpected visitor. He went to Mallwyd and used the phone in the post office to let the people know in Machynlleth.

The locals went up into the hills to see the wreckage and improvised stretchers for the injured crew members using gates lifted from their hinges. All four Germans were taken on a farm trailer to the hospital in Machynlleth, and then sent off to a POW camp in Canada.

In 1985 Kauter returned to Gelli Ddolen to eat jam sandwiches once more. One of his crewmates became a dentist in Caracas in Venezuela.

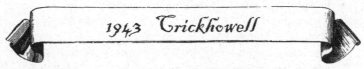

1943 Crickhowell

For All Your Transport Solutions

Muhammad Sakhi is buried in St Edmund's church in Crickhowell, despite not being born there. He actually came from Mang, in the district of Poonch in Kashmir in northern India. Even in death he stands apart. He died on 2 May 1943, aged 24, possibly of influenza, a long way from home. He was part of one of the more unusual units involved in the British Expeditionary Force in France in 1940 – the 32nd Mule Company, part of the Royal Indian Army Service Corps. They were deployed to offer effective transport solutions and they were in fact the first Indian troops to see action.

Initially they were quite useful, despite the extreme cold weather, even though the mules found the icy roads difficult to deal with. It was such an alien environment – weather, landscape, culture, language. The troops were taught to say their name, rank and number in English in case of capture, but otherwise stayed together in their own company. Their duties required them to carry ammunition and supplies to forward positions impassable to wheeled vehicles because of heavy shelling. It was also felt that the mules could do this quietly, especially since they had been 'de-voiced'.

After the German attack in May 1940, the pack transport companies were ordered towards the coast and the 32nd Company became part of the Dunkirk evacuation. It was not possible to ship the mules to England, and they were left in France.

+ During the Second World War, the Home Guard Auxiliary
  Unit based in Carew, Pembrokeshire, was part of a training
  exercise involving a raid on Canadian troops stationed
  in their area to test their readiness and their vigilance.
  The Home Guard invited the Canadians to a local pub
  for drinks on the evening of the raid. Whilst this generous
  hospitality was being enjoyed, some of the auxiliary
  broke into the Canadian camp and removed their combat
  equipment. The next morning the Welsh practice raid was a
  complete success.

+ In April 1940 Mervyn Jones from Cillefwr farm near
  Carmarthen rode the horse Bogskar to victory in the Grand
  National at Aintree. His brother William was riding in the
  same race but he fell from his horse National Night and
  never finished. Both were members of the Royal Air Force.
  Mervyn was lost in action in his Spitfire on a mission over
  Norway in 1942. William was also a fighter pilot; he was
  awarded the Distinguished Flying Cross for his attacks on
  U-boats but he too was lost in action in 1944.

+ It is even stranger to relate that another Grand
  National-winning jockey is buried in Wales and he too
  was a pilot. Robert Everett triumphed on Gregalach in
  1929. Sadly Everett, who was awarded the DSO by King
  George VI in September 1941, was killed on 26 January 1942
  on active service when his Hurricane fighter crashed on
  the beach at Llanddona in Anglesey. He is buried there in
  St Dona's churchyard.

The men were stationed in Crickhowell for a while and then
moved by train to Porthmadog. They camped at Llanfrothen and
Nantmor and practised mountain manoeuvres in preparation
for a possible landing with pack animals in Norway. Their lack of
English was irrelevant, since most of the local people spoke Welsh
anyway. But wherever they went they were treated with interest and
respect – a sudden and unexpected illustration of the extent of the
British Empire.

1943 The Coal Fields

Going Underground

Not all young men served in the armed forces during the Second World War. Some were Bevin Boys and did equally important work underground as miners.

Coal was vital for the war, especially since the Belgian and French coal fields were in German possession. Welsh coal was suddenly important and so, bizarrely, the war brought back prosperity to the valleys.

Mining was made a reserved occupation, exempting miners from military service. The government took over control of the coal industry from its owners and in 1943 the idea of Bevin Boys was introduced, named after the Minister of Labour and

---

+ In the build-up to the D-Day landings in 1944, American troops were based in Swansea. One of them was Rocky Marciano. When he was taunted in the Adelphi club on Wind Street by an Australian serviceman for not drinking alcohol, Marciano knocked him out. There were other incidents too. In the end the military police suggested that he take up amateur boxing to channel the aggression that Swansea seemed to have induced in him. He went on to become undefeated world heavyweight boxing champion.

  At the same time, the legendary boxer Joe Louis fought an exhibition bout in Newport during a morale-boosting visit to US servicemen. So whilst Marciano was on one side of Swansea, Joe Louis was on the other, visiting GIs who were stationed in Morriston.

+ The comedian Frankie Howerd spent part of his wartime service in Penclawwd in Gower.

+ In 1943 a German Fokkewolf fighter plane landed at RAF Pembrey. The confused pilot had convinced himself that he was touching down in occupied France, a mistake that, strangely, few others have made.

National Service. Ten per cent of 18 year olds were drafted down the mines, rather than into the armed forces. It wasn't popular, since the young men involved often felt they were being denied their patriotic duty. Sadly they were often taunted since, without a uniform, they were assumed to be avoiding military service or to be conscientious objectors. They were often stopped and questioned by the police.

Bevin Boys weren't popular with the permanent miners either, because they felt they would take away jobs at the end of the war – and all this in an area where industrial relations had always been a little fragile. Of course the trade unions could never say they were not committed to the war effort, but at the coal face there were tensions. In spite of the war, there were numerous disputes and stoppages – over 500 of them in fact – between 1939 and October 1944. Conditions were grim underground, and there wasn't always much to look forward to on the surface either. In 1944, around 100,000 miners went on strike over pay. As always they fought to protect themselves and their families, in spite of the war, refusing to be abused. But they were beaten with the patriotic stick.

There were also 'pit boy strikes' by young miners in 1942 and 1943, angry at earning less than older men for the same work.

The programme ended in 1948. Their contribution was not acknowledged and they initially received no medals. This was finally rectified in 2008, when survivors received a Veteran's Badge.

 1949 Tredegar Park

Parrot Face

Evan Morgan, the last Viscount Tredegar, was a remarkably bizarre character who died in 1949. He succeeded to the title in 1934 and the status and the income that his title conferred allowed him to indulge his fantasies. And to waste the opportunities that privilege brought him.

He was a poet and a painter, neither with distinction, but with the money he had, talent was never an issue. He was able to pursue a peculiarly indulgent lifestyle.

At Tredegar House in Newport, now by the side of the M4, he kept animals such as a boxing kangaroo in the building itself, along with gorillas and bears. He believed that he was an expert in the occult and had his very own 'Magic Room' where he held peculiar rituals.

Some sources claim his mother, Lady Katherine, had been his role model. They say she believed that she was a bird and built nests throughout the house where she could roost and would be fed seed soaked in sherry by a servant, which all sounds a bit fanciful to me and is certainly not the sort of treatment to which the average battery hen has a chance to become accustomed.

Evan himself was especially fond of his parrot, Blue Boy, and on occasion he encouraged him to climb up inside his trousers and appear through his fly. Yes, I know, that old trick. The bird, which was also perfectly happy to sit upon his shoulder, once pecked Hermann Goering on a nose as a result of a proximity that few others were ever prepared to achieve. Given what you know about him, you will not be surprised to learn that his access to Goering came about because he was a wealthy Nazi sympathiser and close acquaintance of Rudolph Hess.

As an acknowledged homosexual he was twice married. Naturally, one wife was an alleged Russian princess called Olga. He toured Europe's finest hotels with a succession of lovers before converting to Catholicism and becoming chamberlain to Pope Benedict XV and Pius XI. And when he had fulfilled his papal duties he would visit the grave of the poet Percy Shelley in Rome and perform incantations. Papal mass to Black Mass. For Evan, not such a long journey.

He died childless in 1949, the last of the Morgans.

 1949 *Nanteos*

Wooden. You Believe It?

Apparently the Holy Grail, used by Christ at the Last Supper and then again later to gather His blood from the Cross, now lies in a secret bank vault in Wales – a fine twenty-first-century solution to one of the great mysteries of the past.

If you believe in such things, then it was brought to Glastonbury by Joseph of Arimathea and guarded by the monks of the abbey. They ran off with it to Strata Florida during the Dissolution of the

Monasteries and then into the wild hills near Aberystwyth to the manor house of Nanteos, where it was protected and venerated.

It became extremely popular. Drinking water from the Grail would cure anything – and many tested it out. Mind you, there were some pretty desperate people around, because they would bite chunks off it. Today they say that there is only about two thirds of it left.

People could chew it because it was made from wood. You might reasonably expect that the Grail was a precious vessel of beauty, made from gold and studded with precious stones. But no. A piece of the True Cross, if you are really fanatical.

It was on display for a while in the National Museum of Wales, where it was assessed and dated. It is old, certainly, but sadly dates merely from the fourteenth century. But while it might be just a very old drinking vessel mounted in metal, with a band round the rim, believing that it is authentic is all that matters.

So you will believe that it is protected by a guardian, who moves it around to keep it out of the hands of the government? Not that it would do them any good, of course. In the hands of a sinner, it is just a cup. In the hands of a believer it is far more spiritual.

So. Is the Holy Grail guarded by the spirits of the Knights Templar? Is it buried at Glastonbury? Or is it in safety deposit box in a bank in West Wales, sheltered from the Unbelievers?

Tough call.

+ In 1953, the 'Daughters of the American Revolution' erected a plaque enscribed, 'In memory of Prince Madoc, a Welsh explorer who landed on the shores of Mobile Bay in 1170 and left behind, with the Indians, the Welsh language'. It was soon removed by the Alabama Parks Department.

Bibliography

Of course there are lots of resources out there on the Internet these days. But I am from a generation which doesn't believe anything unless it is written in a book. A great deal that relates to the nineteenth and twentieth centuries comes from original sources like newspapers. I have also taken material from the articles I write for *Welsh Country Magazine* but the books below have been extremely helpful. They are proper historians. I am not. I am like Autolycus in Shakespeare's *The Winter's Tale*: 'a snapper up of unconsidered trifles', from the scholarship of others.

Thanks to all of you.

Books

Arnold, Christopher, and Davies, Jeffrey, *Roman and Early Medieval Wales* (The History Press, 2000)

Baring-Gould, S., *Lives of the British Saints* (1907)

Borrow, George, *Wild Wales* (1862)

Breverton, Terry, *100 Great Welshmen* (Glyndŵr Publishing, 2005)

Buchan, John, *Book of Escapes and Hurried Journeys* (Nelson, 1935)

Burrow, Steve, *Shadowland: Wales 3000 – 1500 BC* (Oxbow Books, 2011)

Carradice, Phil, *Snapshots of Welsh History: Without the Boring Bits* (Accent Press, 2011)

Cope, Phil, *Holy Wells: Wales: A Photographic Journey* (Seren, 2008)

Davies, John David, *The History of West Gower* (1877)

de la Bedoyere, Guy, *Roman Towns in Britain* (The History Press, 2003)

Draisey, Derek, *The People of Gower* (Draisey Press, 2003)

Grant, R.K.J., *On the Parish* (Glamorgan Archive Service, 1988)

Hill, Terrence R., *Down in Wales 2: Visits to More Wartime Crash Sites* (Garreg Gwalch, 1996)

Hornsey, Ian Spencer, *A History of Beer and Brewing* (Royal Chemistry Society, 2003)

Howells, W., *Cambrian Superstitions* (1831)

Humphries, John, *Spying for Hitler: The Welsh Double-Cross* (University of Wales Press, 2012)

Knapp, Andrew, and Baldwin, William, *The Newgate Calendar* (London, 1824)

Lambert, W.R., *Drink and Sobriety in Victorian Wales, 1820–95* (University of Wales Press, 1983)

Longmans, Thomas Wright, *A History of Ludlow and its Neighbourhood* (1852)

McCririck, Mary, *Stories of Wales, Book 3* (Gee and Sons, 1963)

Pierce, T. Jones, *Medieval Welsh Society: Selected Essays* (University of Wales Press, 1972)

Rees, Revd Thomas Mardy, *Welsh Painters, Engravers and Sculptors* (Welsh Publishing Company, 1910)

Rees, E.A., *Welsh Outlaws and Bandits: Political Rebellion and Lawlessness, 1400–1603* (Caterwen Press, 2001)

Rees, E.A., *A Life of Guto'r Glyn* (Y Lolfa, 2008)

Richards, D.L., *UFO Wales* (Rossendale Books, 2012)

Roberts, Alun, *Discovering Welsh Graves* (University of Wales Press, 2002)

Roberts, Sara Elin, *Legal Triads of Medieval Wales* (University of Wales Press, 2011)

Sharp, Margaret (ed.), *Accounts of the Constables of Bristol Castle in the Thirteenth and Early Fourteenth Centuries* (Bristol Record Society, 1982)

Smith, Graham, *Smuggling in the Bristol Channel 1700–1850* (Countryside Books, 1989)

Suggett, Richard, *A History of Magic and Witchcraft in Wales* (The History Press, 2008)

Symons, Sarah, *Fortresses and Treasures of Roman Wales* (Breedon Books, 2009)

Tucker, Norman, *Royalist Officers of North Wales 1642–1660* (Norman Tucker, 1961)

Vaughan, Henry Halford, *Welsh Proverbs* (1889)

Vaughan, Sir William, *The Golden Fleece* (1626)

Welsh Book Studies Volume 3 (Aberystwyth, 2000)

Classical and Medieval Texts

Adam of Usk, *Chronicon Adae de Usk, AD 1377–1421*

David Powel, *The Historie of Cambria, now called Wales*

Gerald of Wales, *Descriptio Cambriae*

Jean de Venette, *The Chronicle*

Raphael Holinshed, *Chronicles of England, Scotland and Ireland*

Strabo, *Historical Sketches*

Tacitus, *The Annals*

Other

Hansard (www.parliament.uk/business/publications/hansard)
The Cambrian
The Cardiff and Merthyr Guardian
The Proceedings of the Old Bailey (www.oldbaileyonline.org)
Young, James Carleton, 'Elisabeth, Queen of Roumania', *The Outlook*,
    1 October 1904

And of course, not forgetting

*The Book of Cardiff, Presented to the Delegates at the Annual Conference
    of the National Association of Head teachers* (Oxford University
    Press, 1937)

If you enjoyed this book, you may also be interested in…

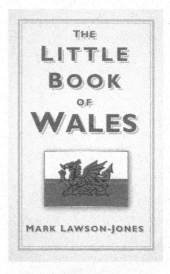

The Little Book of Wales

MARK LAWSON-JONES

This little book is an intriguing, fast-paced, fact-packed compendium of places, people and history in Wales. Discover the country's most unusual crimes and punishments, eccentric inhabitants and hundreds of wacky facts. This can be dipped into time and time again to reveal something new about the people, the heritage, the secrets and the enduring fascination of Wales.

978 0 7524 8927 8

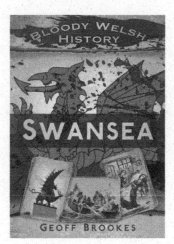

Bloody Welsh History: Swansea

GEOFF BROOKES

Swansea is a place with a dark and murky history. Explore the hidden stories from its long and dangerous past, with tales of rebellion, shipwreck and murder. From Romans to the Red Lady, Viking raids to English attacks, deadly diseases and Nazi bombs – you will never see the city in the same way again.

978 0 7524 8053 4

Visit our website and discover thousands of other History Press books.

www.thehistorypress.co.uk